T0323854

Cambridge Elements

Elements in Politics and Communication
edited by
Stuart Soroka
University of California

ANGRY AND WRONG

The Emotional Dynamics of Partisan Media and Political Misperceptions

Brian E. Weeks
University of Michigan

CAMBRIDGE
UNIVERSITY PRESS

Shaftesbury Road, Cambridge CB2 8EA, United Kingdom

One Liberty Plaza, 20th Floor, New York, NY 10006, USA

477 Williamstown Road, Port Melbourne, VIC 3207, Australia

314–321, 3rd Floor, Plot 3, Splendor Forum, Jasola District Centre,
New Delhi – 110025, India

103 Penang Road, #05–06/07, Visioncrest Commercial, Singapore 238467

Cambridge University Press is part of Cambridge University Press & Assessment,
a department of the University of Cambridge.

We share the University's mission to contribute to society through the pursuit of
education, learning and research at the highest international levels of excellence.

www.cambridge.org
Information on this title: www.cambridge.org/9781009517843

DOI: 10.1017/9781009091121

© Brian E. Weeks 2024

When citing this work, please include a reference to the DOI 10.1017/9781009091121

First published 2024

A catalogue record for this publication is available from the British Library.

ISBN 978-1-009-51784-3 Hardback
ISBN 978-1-009-09509-9 Paperback
ISSN 2633-9897 (online)
ISSN 2633-9889 (print)

Angry and Wrong

The Emotional Dynamics of Partisan Media and Political Misperceptions

Elements in Politics and Communication

DOI: 10.1017/9781009091121
First published online: June 2024

Brian E. Weeks
University of Michigan

Author for correspondence: Brian E. Weeks, beweeks@umich.edu

Abstract: Use of partisan media is often associated with political misperceptions but little research has investigated whether partisan media affect beliefs and, if so, the mechanism through which that process occurs. This Element argues that political anger provides one key theoretical link between partisan media use and political misperceptions. Using three-wave panel survey data collected in the United States during the 2020 election, I show that people who use more partisan media are more angry and misinformed than less frequent or nonusers. More importantly, consuming partisan media – particularly conservative media – can make people angrier about politics over time and this anger subsequently reduces the accuracy of political beliefs. While audiences for partisan media remain small, the findings indicate that these outlets play an important role in shaping political emotions and beliefs and offer one promising explanation for why their audiences are more likely to hold more inaccurate beliefs about politics.

Keywords: Partisan Media, Political Misperceptions, Political Misinformation, Anger, Emotion

ISBNs: 9781009517843 (HB), 9781009095099 (PB), 9781009091121 (OC)
ISSNs: 2633-9897 (online), 2633-9889 (print)

Contents

1 Introduction

As the violent attacks on the United States Capitol unfolded on January 6, 2021, many of the rioters appeared to be driven by two grievances. They expressed anger at the political system, anger at the outcome of the election, and anger at elected officials. At the same time, many rioters that day were motivated by the false belief that the 2020 presidential election was stolen from President Donald Trump through coordinated, systematic voter fraud. They waved signs with allegations of election fraud, chanted slogans like "Stop the Steal," and vowed to fight to take back the country as they stormed the Capitol building.

The events of that day reflect two growing, related trends in American politics; many people are angry about politics and some are misinformed. The sources of anger and misperceptions are complex; decades of declining trust in government, increases in racial resentment, and partisan sorting along ideological, cultural, ethnic, and racial dimensions has made the American public angrier (Phoenix, 2020; Webster, 2020). This anger is rampant throughout the political system in the United States. Politicians use anger as a political strategy to generate support for their campaign or to discredit the opposition (Webster, 2020). Partisan media and online sources of political information use anger-inducing language to describe politics, which can attract audiences, increase engagement with content on social media, and be financially beneficial for the outlet (Berry & Sobieraj, 2013; Hasell, 2021; Hiaeshutter-Rice & Weeks, 2021; Peck, 2020; Young, 2019). The public at large is often angry at people they disagree with politically and willing to express outrage at political opponents (Mason, 2016), a pattern of political hostility that has increased in the United States since the early 2000s (Iyengar et al., 2019). Anger is clearly increasingly prominent in American politics.

At the same time, there is evidence that some Americans are misinformed about the political and social world around them. These political misperceptions, which are defined as personal beliefs that are considered incorrect based on the best available evidence from relevant experts at the time (Vraga & Bode, 2020), are a significant element of contemporary politics in the United States. Although there is some debate about the degree to which the American public is truly misinformed (Graham, 2023), there is no question that misinformation, disinformation, false conspiracy theories, and rumors are often believed.[1] One need only

---

[1] Misinformation and disinformation are sometimes distinguished in the literature by the intention behind false information, with misinformation considered unintentionally false information and disinformation being intentionally or purposefully false information (Jack, 2017). Conspiracy theories are attempts to explain social and political events with claims of secret plots by powerful actors (Douglas et al., 2019). While there are subtle nuances in these concepts, for the purposes of this book I primarily use the term "misinformation" to describe all false information and the label "misperceptions" to note false beliefs.

to look at polls registering Americans' false beliefs to see the potential threat misperceptions pose to politics and society. Two years after the 2020 US presidential election, surveys indicate that nearly one-third of Americans do not believe President Joe Biden legitimately won the election (Monmouth University, 2022). One in four Americans believed that Covid-19 was a planned conspiracy (Pew, 2020). Misperceptions are prevalent and problematic.

The simultaneous prominence of anger and misperceptions is not a coincidence. On the one hand, anger can make people more partisan and less rational. Anger can lead people to turn to political information sources that reinforce existing beliefs. It can encourage them to ignore, downplay, or counterargue evidence that challenges their worldview (MacKuen et al., 2010). Ultimately, anger can make people more susceptible to believing false claims about politics, science, and health if those claims are consistent with their political or ideological views (Weeks, 2015). On the other hand, much of the political mis- and disinformation in the public sphere directly plays on people's anger about the political world. The goal of much political disinformation, in fact, is to stoke anger about cultural, political, ideological, racial, or religious differences in society. Given the concurrent prevalence of anger and misperceptions in American politics, I argue that they are inextricably linked; anger promotes misperceptions and misperceptions fuel anger. The big question is, what is making us so angry and so often wrong about politics?

The power and prevalence of anger and false beliefs highlight the need to understand how such feelings develop and persist among the public. Certainly, in the case of beliefs about election fraud in 2020, partisan polarization coupled with consistent claims perpetuated by Donald Trump added to the outrage and misperceptions. There's little question that partisan sorting, growing distrust in institutions like government and media, along with active attempts by nationalist and foreign actors to undermine democratic societies have fueled both anger and misperceptions (Bennett & Livingston, 2018; Jamieson, 2020). But other causes may be responsible as well. Notably, partisan media outlets – which tend to explicitly favor one political party or ideology over the other – may also contribute to both anger and false beliefs in American society. For example, consider the case of false beliefs about voter fraud in the 2020 US presidential election. It is notable that in 2020 and early 2021, *Fox News* – which is considered conservative partisan media – aired hundreds of television segments that mentioned voter or election fraud (Television Archive, n.d.). While not all mentions explicitly claimed that voter fraud took place during the election, some of the references suggested that election misconduct was at work and that allegations of fraud had merit. Such references to voter fraud may have angered audiences of conservative partisan media and promoted beliefs that election fraud was widespread.

The potential link between partisan media, anger, and misperceptions is not limited to Republican- or conservative-leaning media. During the 2020 presidential campaign there were claims circulating on social media that Donald Trump conspired with Postmaster General Louis DeJoy to deliberately slow down mail delivery service to undermine mail-in voting and help Trump win the election. While mail did slow down after DeJoy assumed his post, the claim that Trump directed the move for political gain was not supported by evidence (Lee, 2020). This claim drew ire among Democrats and was reported by liberal-leaning partisan media outlets. For example, a *Daily Kos* headline from July 31, 2020 read "Trump's Scheme to Hobble Vote-by-Mail in Full Swing Under Top GOP Donor-Turned-Postmaster General." That same day, *MSNBC* host Rachel Maddow took to Facebook to note that "There's a 'growing perception' that U.S. Postal Service delays are the result of a 'political effort' to undermine voting by mail" despite any concrete evidence of such efforts.

What these examples illustrate is that partisan media exposure, political anger, and political misperceptions may be closely linked. Existing evidence indicates that they are indeed related. My prior research shows that frequent users of partisan media are more angry than those who rarely or do not use partisan media (Hasell & Weeks, 2016), that political anger promotes false beliefs (Weeks, 2015), and that use of partisan media is associated with more political misperceptions (Garrett et al., 2016; Weeks et al., 2023). These individual pieces point to the power of partisan media to anger and misinform audiences but a larger, more expansive test of the causal role of partisan media, as well as how this process unfolds over time is needed. Open questions persist: are partisan media at least partially responsible for the anger and misinformation that have come to characterize the political system in the United States? If so, do conservative and liberal partisan media exert the same degree of influence on audiences?

The answers to these questions are critically important, particularly given unsettled debates about the influence partisan media have in contemporary American politics and society. Some critics argue that partisan media play a damaging role in American politics, allowing people to use extreme, partisan media at the expense of more moderate, nonpartisan news (Sunstein, 2007). The concern here is that people will fall into media ecosystems where the only information they see reinforces their existing worldviews, polarizing and misinforming them along the way. Others have challenged this argument and suggest instead that the influence of partisan media is more minimal, particularly given that partisan audiences are small. The overwhelming majority of

Americans do not use partisan media on a regular basis; most Americans have somewhat diverse news repertoires and do not exist in like-minded echo chambers or filter bubbles online (see Arguedas et al., 2022; Jamieson et al., 2023). In fact, audiences for partisan sources remain quite small relative to other, more mainstream news outlets (Guess, 2021). This would suggest that partisan media may appeal to smaller, more fringe audiences that are not reflective of the larger public. Because these audiences remain relatively small, the argument suggests, partisan media are not capable of creating widespread polarization and discord present in the American political system (Prior, 2013; Wojcieszak et al., 2023). Yet a third possibility remains: partisan media audiences are small but democratically troublesome. While direct audiences are modest, angry and misinformed users of partisan media still raise alarm, particularly given the disproportionate influence they potentially have on American politics through their activities on- and offline (Prior, 2013). More evidence of the impact of partisan media is clearly needed.

The purpose of this Element is to better understand if and how partisan media affect false political beliefs by more systematically examining the relationships between partisan media exposure, political anger, and political misperceptions during the 2020 U S presidential election. To do so, I rely on a comprehensive survey of 1,800 American adults who closely resemble the population of the United States and were surveyed at three time periods in the fall of 2020. The survey measured their media exposure – including partisan media – along with their levels of political anger and their beliefs about a series of false claims related to politics, science, and health that were circulating at that time. By surveying the same group of respondents three times during the election season, the data allow me to more precisely test how partisan media introduce, change, and/or reinforce levels of political anger over time. The data here can also be used to examine whether partisan media exposure and political anger bias political beliefs, making people more likely to accept political falsehoods as true. The three waves of data also allow me to test whether people who are angry and/or misinformed are subsequently drawn to partisan media over time, which may further reinforce anger and misperceptions (Slater, 2007). This approach therefore offers a more stringent causal test of the reciprocal influence of partisan media on anger and misperceptions.

Through these analyses, I find that partisan media matter a great deal. They are influential in shaping their audiences' anger and beliefs about politics. These effects are persistent even when accounting for other explanations, like political party identification or ideology. Although the audiences for these outlets are relatively small, the people who consistently use partisan media think, feel, and behave differently from those who infrequently or do not use them. Compared to people who are not (or rarely) exposed to ideological media, users of partisan media are angrier at their political opponents and are considerably more willing to believe political falsehoods that reflect well on their own political party or poorly on the opposing party. There is also evidence that the relationships here are often mutually reinforcing; partisan media incite anger and misperceptions, which make it even more likely that audiences seek out these sources again in the future. Such a reinforcing spiral may make it difficult to combat false beliefs, or diminish feelings of political anger, and point to the power partisan media can hold over audiences.

However, the analyses that follow show that the role of partisan media in the United States is asymmetrical and different depending on the ideological alignment of the source. In short, the data indicate that conservative partisan media have a stronger and more consistent impact on audiences' anger and misperceptions than do liberal media. During the 2020 election, users of conservative partisan media became more angry and inaccurate in their beliefs over time and were angrier and more misinformed than those who used conservative partisan media infrequently or not at all. This suggests that conservative media can *cause* people to be more angry and misinformed. Similarly, audiences of liberal partisan media were also angrier and held more false beliefs than did people who did not use it frequently. But there is little evidence in the data that users of liberal partisan media became more angry and misinformed during the election as a result of using these sources. While both types of media are no doubt important in shaping audiences' beliefs, conservative and liberal partisan media are not equivalent in their effects on the American public. Rather, conservative media are particularly influential in promoting anger and political misperceptions among their audiences.

This Element proceeds as follows: in the next section, I draw on theories of media exposure, emotion, and information processing to outline my expectations regarding the ways in which partisan media promote anger and misperceptions. Along the way I argue that anger is the vital link between exposure to partisan news and being misinformed; partisan media trigger anger in their audiences, which subsequently promotes incorrect beliefs. After outlining the theory, I next describe the survey and data before reporting my analyses. I conclude by offering a discussion of the implications of findings.

2 How Partisan Media Drive Anger and Misperceptions

2.1 What Are 'Partisan' Media?

One defining feature of the contemporary American political media environment is the prevalence of explicitly partisan political information sources. Partisan media outlets are those that present political information in a way that is notably favorable to one political party or ideology (Levendusky, 2013). The partisan nature of this coverage is evident in a few ways; outlets can be partisan (and biased) both in the types of stories they cover or the way in which they frame or emphasize certain aspects of an issue (Baum & Groeling, 2008; Jamieson & Cappella, 2008). Partisan media can be distinguished from mainstream or nonpartisan news outlets that follow the norms and routines of professional journalism, providing general-interest content that is produced through processes of accurate reporting, fact-checking, editing, and institutional oversight. These often include large national newspapers, broadcast television outlets, and public media. Partisan outlets, in contrast, do not always follow these procedures. Instead, they often market themselves or are perceived by audiences or third parties as correctives to or in opposition to more traditional, mainstream news sources. Much of their content, which often relies on highly opinionated commentary rather than original reporting (Levendusky, 2013), directly challenges or offers a counternarrative to what is provided by more mainstream news outlets (Holt et al., 2019).

Technological changes and widespread adoption of the internet have allowed partisan media to grow over the last thirty years in the United States. Following the success of conservative talk radio hosts like Rush Limbaugh in the late 1980s and early 1990s, the expansion of cable news allowed partisan television networks like *Fox News*, which was launched in 1996, to build an audience and become a prominent voice in American politics (Brock et al., 2012; Hemmer, 2016; Jamieson & Cappella, 2008; Peck, 2020). Over the past twenty-five years, *Fox News* has become one of the most popular news brands in the United States by offering explicitly conservative partisan content intended to appeal to and attract a right-leaning audience. The data suggests it is working. According to a 2020 Pew Poll, *Fox News* was the most commonly cited source for political and election news among the American public, as 16% of US adults named *Fox News* as their main source for election news and nearly 40% reported getting news from *Fox* in the prior week. Two-thirds of Republicans named *Fox News* as their most-trusted news source (Pew, 2020a; Pew, 2020b). Although not nearly as successful as *Fox News*, liberal partisan outlets like *MSNBC* have also become commonplace in the American media environment.

But partisan media outlets are not limited to cable television brands like *Fox News* or *MSNBC*. On the political right, an ecosystem of influential right-wing media outlets has emerged that do not always adhere to norms of journalistic objectivity or engage in fact and evidence-based reporting (Benkler et al., 2018). These sites have become some of the most popular and influential political information outlets on the internet. In many cases, right-wing media outlets have a comparable (or even more) number followers on social media platforms like Facebook than do more mainstream, national news outlets. For example, the *Daily Caller* (6.2 million) and the *Washington Post* (7.3 million) have roughly similar numbers of followers. On both the right and left, podcasters, influencers, and YouTubers have joined the ranks of popular partisan media. Some of these individuals also have relatively large followings online. Hasan Piker, for instance, is a progressive political commentator who has more than 2.5 million followers on the streaming platform, Twitch. While partisan media have historically been thought of as "news," the universe of media content that falls under this umbrella is growing, rapidly changing, and, potentially, financially lucrative.

While partisan media exists on both the right and left, conservative and liberal partisan media are not equivalent. As I argue, there are important distinctions in terms of their popularity, content, and effects. Conservative media in particular play an important role in the American political media ecosystem. Starting with the success of Rush Limbaugh and *Fox News,* conservative media outlets have come to explicitly brand themselves as a counter or alternative to more mainstream media, which is often portrayed in conservative media as untrustworthy, liberal, and excessively out of touch with working, middle-class (White) Americans and their values (Brock et al., 2012; Peck, 2020). This populist and angry rhetoric caught on and attracted audiences to conservative media both off- and online (Young, 2019). Although many do not use these sites exclusively, more than six in ten Republicans report getting news from *Fox News* every week (Pew, 2021). No liberal source attracts Democratic audiences in the same way. Conservative news has also become quite prominent online and on social media. Right-wing news sites online have created a tight-knit media ecosystem in which conservative content – including misinformation – is shared and amplified in a way that is insulated from more moderate or centrist news sites (Benkler et al., 2018). This conservative media ecosystem does not have a liberal equivalent or a mirrored system on the left. Such asymmetries in conservative and liberal news exposure are apparent on social media as well. There is evidence of ideological segregation on platforms like Facebook, as sources favored by conservative audiences are more prominent on the platform than liberal ones. Further, a small group of very conservative users tend to frequently use right-leaning pages on the platform, isolating themselves from more centrist content (González-Bailón et al., 2023). As I note later, the popularity and influence of conservative partisan media may have important consequences for audiences' beliefs about science, health, and politics.

2.2 Who Uses Partisan Media and Why?

As the internet and social media expanded in the late twentieth and early twenty-first centuries, some critics raised concerns that technological changes to the media environment would provide people the opportunity to create news and political information diets that reflect their personal beliefs, partisan affiliations, or political ideologies, while also avoiding sources that challenged their political views or were more politically neutral (e.g. Sunstein, 2007). These concerns – whether called filter bubble, echo chambers, or media balkanization – were based in part on the theory of selective exposure, which suggests that people prefer news and information outlets that reinforce their existing political views because those sources often tell people what they want to hear, while avoiding or downplaying uncomfortable political truths (Stroud, 2011). If taken to the extreme, technology can facilitate the construction of 'echo chambers' in which news consumers only expose themselves to news and political information from sources that are politically congenial. Similarly, algorithmic filtering based on political and content preferences could help construct filter bubbles of politically aligned information online (Pariser, 2011). At the center of these processes are partisan media outlets.

Although a popular media and political narrative suggests that most Americans are creating echo-chambers by self-selecting into like-minded partisan media, *this claim is not supported by the evidence.* Over the past twenty years, hundreds of studies have been conducted to test the extent to which people only expose themselves to politically like-minded partisan news. An abundance of evidence suggests people prefer like-minded content but don't actively avoid information they disagree with (Garrett, 2009). In fact, many people consume no news at all and few people consistently use only like-minded partisan media (Guess, 2021). Studies that track individuals' internet use in the United States by evaluating browser histories indicate that less 2% of all website visits online are to news sites and only 0.75% are to explicitly partisan media sites (Wojcieszak et al., 2023). Further, the evidence indicates those who do consume like-minded partisan news tend not to avoid other more neutral or even disagreeable news sources. All told, recent estimates suggest that less than 5% of Americans are in online news echo chambers. For comparison, approximately 30% of Americans consume no online news at all (Fletcher et al., 2021; Jamieson et al., 2023). This is not to say that echo chambers are nonexistent; recent evidence suggests that a small but perhaps growing segment of conservative news audiences exist in echo chambers (Benkler et al., 2018; González-Bailón et al., 2023; Guess, 2021; Jamieson et al., 2023). But little evidence supports the notion that most people exist in partisan echo chambers.

While only a very small percentage of the American population exists in echo chambers, this does not mean that people are not at times exposed to partisan media. The contemporary information environment allows people to be exposed to partisan content in a number of ways. Consumers can actively seek out partisan media by watching partisan cable television channels like *Fox News*, visiting partisan websites, or following partisan media sources on social media. In addition to these active approaches, people can also be incidentally exposed to partisan content without purposefully seeking it. While algorithms employed by social media platforms like Facebook or remain a proprietary black box, we do know that they prioritize and amplify content that receives engagement from other users. This amplification of engaged content has enabled partisan media to thrive on social media platforms. Users engage more frequently with content from partisan outlets (relative to nonpartisan outlets) on social media platforms, particularly more extreme conservative pages. Posts from partisan media pages on Facebook receive far more user engagement in the form of likes, comments, and shares than do more mainstream sources. The most popular conservative media outlets on Facebook received, on average, approximately 10,000 likes and 5,000 shares per post. The most engaged mainstream pages, in comparison, received roughly 5,000 likes and 2,000 shares for each post (Hiashutter-Rice & Weeks, 2021). Content from partisan media, especially when it contains angry language, outpaces mainstream media in the number of shares and retweets on Twitter as well (Hasell, 2021). These partisan sites are also shared widely by other, like-minded media outlets, which can expand their reach even further (Benkler et al., 2018). People may also be exposed to rumors and false content from partisan sites via online searches (Weeks & Southwell, 2010). While the majority of people may not actively use partisan media, people clearly still encounter partisan media content through more passive exposure via online social networks (Druckman et al., 2018; Hasell, 2021; Thorson & Wells, 2016).

Such stark differences in engagement between partisan and mainstream media outlets raises the questions of why people are drawn to these outlets and why their content is amplified so widely, despite the relatively small, immediate audience. In terms of exposure, partisan media provide political content that often explicitly appeals to people who share the outlets' political values or worldview. Research on selective exposure indicates that people are often psychologically attached to news sources and information that reinforce their existing political attitudes and beliefs (Garrett, 2009; Stroud, 2011). Although most people do not systematically avoid content or sources that challenge their worldview, they do have a strong preference for like-minded content, which partisan media delivers (Garrett & Stroud, 2014). Many users of partisan media turn to these outlets likely because they get messages highlighting the positives of their political or social groups, alongside messages that criticize and denounce political opponents, all of which serve to reinforce existing political and social identities (Young, 2023).

Preference for politically like-minded content is not the only explanation for why people use partisan media for political information; partisan media users also tend to find those sources more credible than mainstream sources (Guess et al, 2021; Metzger et al., 2020; Tsfati & Cappella, 2003). As people increasingly distrust government and institutions (Bennett & Livingston, 2018), there is also a growing perception among many Americans – particularly conservatives and Republicans – that mainstream media are biased, corrupt, or don't reflect the values of certain segments of the population (Holt et al., 2019). Partisan media provide many of these individuals an alternative outlet for political content and information that they find more credible, in part because it often tells them what they want to hear.

2.3 Partisan Media Content

Partisan media are information outlets that tend to cover news and politics in a way that unfairly favors one political party or ideology over others, and that the coverage is opinionated rather than based on facts and evidence (Levendusky, 2013). As previously mentioned, the embrace of one political ideology can emerge either through the political stories outlets choose to cover or how they frame topics (Baum & Groeling, 2008).

In terms of story selection, partisan media can choose to cover and emphasize topics and issues that favor the political party, ideology, or politician(s) with which they are aligned. For example, both Democratic and Republican-leaning outlets tend to provide more coverage of political scandals that involve political opponents than scandals that involve ideologically-aligned politicians (Puglisi & Snyder, 2011). To examine if this trend continued in recent years, I used the Internet Archive for TV news (see archive.org/details/tv) to search cable news transcripts for mentions of two political scandals from the 2020 US presidential election. The first scandal – which was likely more appealing to conservative audiences – involved the unproven claim that President Joe Biden and his son, Hunter, were involved in corruption surrounding business dealings in Ukraine. The second scandal involved the unproven claim that former US president Donald Trump purposely slowed down the US mail system in order to delay mail in ballots, thus giving Trump an electoral advantage. A rough search of the Internet Archive provided evidence of story bias; between September 1 and Election Day (November 3), 2020 *Fox News* mention Hunter Biden significantly more than did *CNN*. The same pattern emerged for liberal partisan sources and the Trump claim; *MSNBC* and *CNN* mentioned Trump and the US mail considerably more than did *Fox News*. I provide more detail on these differences in later chapters but for now suffice it to say that partisan outlets offer divergent levels of coverage to political rumors, falsehoods, and scandals, depending in part on the outlet's ideology.

Not only do partisan media outlets cover different (un)favorable stories to different degrees, they also use production mechanisms to emphasize or deemphasize different political topics (Shultziner & Stukalin, 2021). For example, a minor gaffe by a Democratic politician may be a prominently-placed story on a conservative partisan media site whereas serious allegations against Republican politicians like former President Trump may be placed where readers need to scroll extensively to see it.

In addition to story selection and presentation, partisan media also tend to cover or frame stories in ways that favor one political ideology, viewpoint, or group over others. Despite often positioning themselves as unbiased or, in the case of *Fox News*, "Fair and Balanced," partisan media are opinionated media (Levendusky, 2013) and in many instances are explicit in their partisan bias, though these biases can be implicit too. Although ideological differences in news coverage between some partisan and mainstream sources may not be as vast as expected, audiences see opinionated content from right-leaning sources as conservative and opinionated content from left-leaning sources as liberal (Budak et al., 2016). Such biases are therefore evident and perceptible to audiences. For example, coverage of the second impeachment trial of Donald Trump differed wildly in liberal and conservative outlets. Political commentators on *CNN* and *MSNBC* praised the trial, describing it as an important moment of American political accountability. In contrast, the trial was described on conservative partisan media like *Fox News* and *Newsmax* as "asinine," "offensive," and "absurd" (Hsu & Robertson, 2021). These very different presentations of the same events highlight that partisan media can leave people with contrasting pictures of the world, depending on where they learn about an issue or topic.

Not only is opinionated content from partisan media perceived as either liberal or conservative, but the way these sources frame and cover political topics differs from nonpartisan sources. For example, conservative partisan media cover issues like immigration in a way that is remarkably different than nonpartisan media. A content analyses of news coverage of undocumented migration to the United States at the southern border found that conservative media outlets like *Fox News*, compared to nonpartisan outlets, were more likely to emphasize the crime and criminality of immigration than were nonpartisan sources, were less likely to discuss the morality of the issue, and featured more visuals of immigrants running or trying to climb fences at the border (Famulari, 2020). Similar differences in coverage have been found on other topics, like climate change. A content analyses of climate change news coverage on partisan cable television in the United States found that *Fox News* was considerably more dismissive of the existence of climate change than were *CNN* or *MSNBC* and that *Fox News* was also significantly more likely to ignore or even reject the scientific consensus surrounding climate change than were the more liberal outlets (Feldman et al., 2012). Partisan media – on both the right and left – actively criticize mainstream media as well. While conservative media often denounce mainstream media, liberal partisan commentators are also highly critical of mainstream news and attempt to sow distrust in these mainstream news organizations among their audiences (Guess et al., 2021; Peck, 2023).

Differences in content between conservative and liberal partisan media are also apparent in the degree to which they cover and spread political misinformation. Notably, there is growing evidence that conservative media devotes extensive attention to political falsehoods. For example, during the 2020 US presidential election, conservative media further amplified Donald Trump's false claim that the election was stolen and that the outcome was fraudulent (Jamieson et al., 2023). Three of the most covered issues on *Fox News* during the 2020 election centered on unsubstantiated stories about Joe Biden's support for "extreme" racial ideologies, mail-in voting fraud, and the (lack of) severity of Covid-19 (Broockman & Kalla, 2023). On social media, a high volume of political misinformation on platforms like Facebook exist in pockets of highly conservative pages, more so than on liberal pages (González-Bailón et al., 2023). Misinformation also appears to spread through networks of conservative partisan media in way that is not mirrored by more liberal media (Benkler et al., 2018). Audiences of conservative partisan news may therefore be exposed to more false or misleading information than audiences of liberal or mainstream media. This exposure appears to influence the beliefs of audiences as well; use of conservative partisan media is associated with greater acceptance of misinformation about political, scientific, and health issues, relative to use of liberal partisan media (Feldman et al., 2014; Garrett et al., 2016; Garrett et al., 2019; Meirick, 2013; Weeks et al., 2023).

The nature of political coverage in partisan outlets has implications for how audiences react emotionally to this content. As noted, the majority of Americans do not extensively use partisan media (Guess, 2021; Prior, 2013; Wojcieszak et al., 2023) but those who do are often different from their peers who do not frequently use partisan news; users of partisan media often hold more extreme attitudes that are more consistent with their partisanship or ideology

(Hmielowski et al., 2020; Levendusky, 2013; Stroud, 2011). Teasing out a causal influence is challenging because we know that some individuals self-select into like-minded partisan media sources, making it difficult to determine whether any observed differences are attributable to partisan media content or preexisting partisan beliefs (Prior, 2013). Nonetheless, experimental research indicates that exposure to partisan media – especially when individuals choose to expose themselves to this content – can shape attitudes and beliefs and further polarize audiences (e.g. Arceneaux & Johnson, 2013; Levendusky, 2013).

2.4 Partisan Media Can Anger and Misinform Audiences

A market strategy of partisan media has been to trigger outrage and anger in their audiences (Berry & Sobieraj, 2013; Mutz, 2016; Young, 2019). Anger can be financially lucrative for media outlets; emotions like anger can increase attention to political media outlets, increase the time audiences spend with these outlets, and encourage engagement with their content (Bakir & McStay, 2018), all of which can increase revenue. Partisan media generate anger by relying heavily on news features, stories, and issues that are known to elicit emotions in audiences, including attack-oriented content, scandals, corruption, provocative headlines, unflattering images, and evocative graphics (e.g. Hasell et al., 2024; Roberts & Wahl-Jorgensen, 2022). This, coupled with the fact that news media have generally become more emotional in their presentation style over time, including more storytelling and the dramatization of news (Wahl-Jorgensen, 2019) suggests partisan media may be particularly likely to induce emotions like anger.

Anger has always been an important emotion for politics (Marcus et al., 2000). It is a discrete, negative, but motivating emotion that emerges when people perceive an offense or injustice has occurred (Carver & Harmon-Jones, 2009); partisan media seem to be uniquely suited to cultivate such anger. Anger can arise in the audience if news coverage suggests a perceived offense to the individual or their social group, or if news coverage blames an individual or social group for some perceived unjust event (Arpan & Nabi, 2011; Goodall et al., 2013; Nabi, 2003). For example, *Fox News* often exhibits a populist style of news coverage that emphasizes social, economic, racial, and political divisions in society in a way that promotes anger and group-based polarization (Broockman & Kalla, 2023; Peck, 2019), in part by making individuals' political and social identities more salient to them (Young, 2023). This is reflected in the social media strategies of partisan media as well. Social media posts from partisan media pages are more likely to express anger than are posts from mainstream news (Hasell, 2021), suggesting partisan media explicitly use anger in their content to attract audiences. Partisan media also often engage in or highlight political attacks on opponents and display other types of political incivility (Mutz, 2016; Young, 2019), which can promote anger and other negative feelings, like cynicism (Hasell & Weeks, 2016; Hasell et al., 2024). In fact, audiences may turn to partisan media for the explicit purpose of experiencing outrage at the other side, or for finding justification for their existing political anger (Boyer, 2023; Song, 2017; Young, 2019).

There is evidence that partisan media do in fact trigger emotional responses, particularly anger. People who consistently use partisan media are more angry about politics than their peers who don't use these outlets as often (Hasell & Weeks, 2016; Lu & Lee, 2019; Wojcieszak et al., 2016). Users of partisan media also tend to express more general negative emotions and affect toward political opponents (Garrett et al., 2019). This suggests that emotionally evocative coverage in partisan media can affect how the audience feels about politics and political figures more broadly.

Taken together, partisan media are likely to encourage anger but there are several reasons to expect that they will also promote political misperceptions. First, because partisan media are often biased and favorable toward some political parties, ideologies, or groups over others, they may discuss false or misleading claims that provide a strategic advantage to the supported party. This coverage is sometimes designed with the explicit purpose of creating confusion, misunderstandings, or misperceptions about individuals, groups, or policies (Bennett & Livingston, 2018; Faris et al., 2017; Garrett et al., 2016; Jamieson & Cappella, 2008; Marwick & Lewis, 2017; Vargo et al., 2018). For example, during the 2016 US presidential election, *Fox News* heavily covered unsubstantiated allegations and scandals surrounding Hillary Clinton's campaign, and 95% of this coverage was negative (Patterson, 2016). Such coverage can promote belief in misleading or false claims by connecting the information to people's own political identities. When political identities are primed in this way, people are more likely to accept falsehoods that are consistent with their worldview (Young, 2023), particularly falsehoods about political opponents (Flynn et al., 2017).

Second, partisan media do not need to explicitly share and spread misinformation in order to misinform. In many cases, the influence of partisan media on beliefs is more subtle. In particular, partisan media may work to discredit and undermine experts and expert conclusions, which can promote political falsehoods. Studies suggest that users of partisan media are no less knowledgeable about expert conclusions surrounding political, scientific, and health issues. However, people who use partisan media are more likely to misunderstand or even outright reject what experts believe, leading to greater levels of misperceptions (Garrett et al., 2016). Such dynamics can help explain why users of partisan media were more misinformed about Covid-19 prevention behaviors, including vaccines, and were less likely to engage in those preventative actions (Motta & Stecula, 2023; Motta et al., 2020). If doctors and medical experts are routinely discredited in partisan media, audiences may begin to question their expertise or recommendations.

Third, and most importantly, partisan media can misinform via the anger they elicit in their audience. Partisan media tend to emphasize differences between social and political groups, which can make people more aware of their own identities and promote feelings of anger at the political system or opponents (Young, 2023; Weeks, 2023). Anger is a powerful emotion in shaping political beliefs; it can make people see and think about the world in a more partisan way. Angry people tend behave in a more partisan manner and use more partisan biases when they engage with political information (MacKuen et al., 2010; Marcus et al., 2000). Notably, angry people are more likely to engage in partisan motivated reasoning and exhibit political biases when considering the veracity of political information; when people experience high-arousal negative emotions (like anger), they are more likely to counterargue identity-challenging information and are less willing to extend support to political outgroups (Boyer, 2023).

These findings suggest anger can reduce effortful information processing and lead people to engage in less careful, considerate, and deliberate thought, and instead rely more on partisan heuristics in their judgement and decision-making (Webster, 2020). These emotional dynamics can help explain why people tend to believe falsehoods about politics, science, and health, particularly when they are aligned with individuals' political worldview or ideology. Anger can make people rely on their party identity when forming political beliefs, which can leave them more vulnerable to believing claims that are not true if those beliefs reflect well on their political party (Carnahan et al., 2023). Angry people are more likely to ignore facts and evidence that challenges their identities or worldviews and find inaccurate information more credible if it supports their prior views (see Weeks, 2023 for review). For example, in an experimental study, I found that angry people were more likely to believe false information about immigration if those falsehoods came from a politician from their own political party (Weeks, 2015). In other words, angry people are very willing to believe political falsehoods if those falsehoods align with their worldview. If partisan media are able to trigger anger, their audiences should be more susceptible to believing false claims that favor their side politically.

2.5 Reinforcing Spirals: Partisan Media, Anger, and Misperceptions

We know from prior research that people who use partisan media are more angry and misinformed, and also that angry people are more likely to believe political falsehoods. The analyses that follow test these relationships in a larger, more comprehensive model that examines the process over time. Importantly, it attempts to provide a much-needed answer to the question of why we find considerable evidence that partisan media audiences are misinformed, despite consuming so much political news and information. I argue that anger is the key here; partisan media increase anger in their audience, which subsequently influences what those audiences believe about politics. In this case, anger can lead people to believe claims about politics that are not true.

Theoretically, I rely on what is known as the reinforcing spirals model (RSM) of political media effects (Slater, 2007). The crux of the RSM is that media effects do not exist in a vacuum, independent of personal characteristics, identities, emotions, and worldviews that people bring to any engagement with or selection of media. Rather, the theory argues that people's existing identities, attitudes, emotions, and/or beliefs influence what media they consume. In particular, people are more likely to select media content that reinforces existing worldviews. Exposure to that media content subsequently strengthens those existing attitudes, identities, emotions, beliefs, etc., making it even more likely that people continue to use self-reinforcing media in the future (Hmielowski et al., 2020). In this way, media selection and effects are dynamic processes in which identities, attitudes, emotions, and beliefs affect which media people choose to consume, which serves to maintain, reinforce, or strengthen those concepts over time (Shehata et al., 2024; Slater, 2007).

The RSM provides a framework to understand the dynamics and associations between partisan media use, political anger, and political misperceptions. It allows me to make predictions for how these concepts influence each other over time. Based on the RSM, I argue that use of partisan media reinforces both political anger and misperceptions. More specifically, politically angry and misinformed individuals will be more likely to use partisan media in the first place. Using partisan media should, over time, further increase levels of political anger and acceptance of political falsehoods, which will in turn promote even more partisan media use. While the RSM is often employed to understand the relationships between media use and social or political identities, the model can also be utilized to understand over-time effects of media use, emotions, and beliefs (Slater, 2007).

Importantly, the RSM enables me to examine change both within and between individuals over time (Thomas et al., 2021). For example, to what extent do individuals who use partisan media see changes in anger and misperceptions? In other words, do users of partisan media become more angry and misinformed over time? The RSM model also allows for predictions in differences between individuals. That is, are the people who frequently use partisan media more angry and misinformed than the people who do not?

These predictions are depicted visually in Figure 1, with the corresponding path noted in the figure and the text later. The paths in the center part of the model (paths a though f) represent within-person effects. That is, to what extent do individuals' partisan media use, anger, and misperceptions influence each other and change over time? Were relationships evident here, this would suggest that partisan media content is changing what people feel and believe. The paths at the outer part of the model (g, h, i) represent between-person effects, which illustrate how the extent to which people use partisan media (e.g. frequent vs. rare use) influences anger and false beliefs.

It is necessary to highlight three important distinctions about these predictions. First, I expect the effects of partisan media to be on anger and beliefs about politicians and issues *the outlet opposes*. For example, I expect users of conservative partisan media to be more angry and misinformed about Biden (and not Trump) and vice versa for users of liberal partisan media. I would not expect, for example, that using liberal media would increase anger or misperceptions about Biden and the same is true with using conservative media and feelings and beliefs about Trump.

Second, this approach means that I test the effects of conservative and liberal partisan media separately. Some evidence suggests that conservative partisan media may be more prominent and politically influential than liberal partisan media (e.g. Benkler et al., 2018; Garrett et al., 2016; González-Bailón et al., 2023; Weeks et al., 2023), though other work finds symmetry in the influence of conservative and liberal media (see Hmielowski et al., 2020). Clearly, more attention to this question is needed. One question I examine is whether there are asymmetrical effects of conservative and liberal media on political anger and misperceptions.

Third, note that I am not strictly testing the effects of selective exposure. I don't stipulate or examine who is using partisan media or how they arrived at these sites. Rather, I am interested in all individuals' exposure to partisan media, including passive, incidental exposure. We know that people can be inadvertently exposed to partisan content through social networks and algorithmic filtering. While, for example, the influence of partisan media may be greater for like-minded partisans who self-select into this content, I am more interested in how *anyone* who encounters these sources reacts to partisan content. In other words, I am not examining the effect of exposure to like-minded political

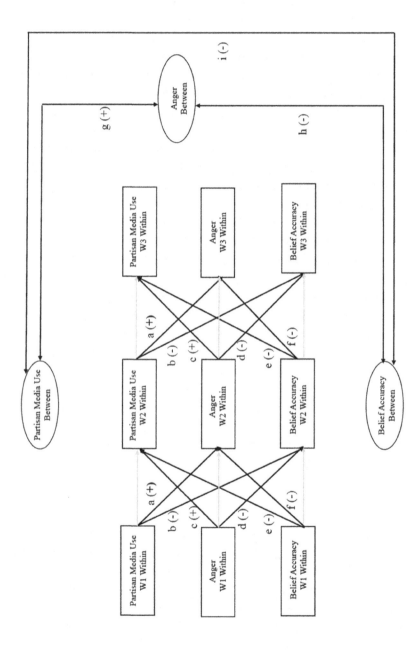

Figure 1 Hypothesized within- and between-person relationships between partisan media use, political anger, and belief accuracy across three waves.

content, but instead I am examining the effect of partisan media on all individuals who are exposed to them. Because of this, the tests below are in some ways more conservative because they are not simply looking at the effects of people who seek out like-minded content, but rather the audiences of partisan media as a whole. With this in mind, and incorporating both within- and between-person effects noted earlier, I expect the following:

1. Users of partisan media will become more angry at the outlets' political opponents over time (a path) and frequency of use will be positively associated with political anger (g path).
2. Users of partisan media will become more politically misinformed over time (b path) and frequency of use will be negatively associated with belief accuracy (i.e. more misperceptions) (i path).
3. People who are angry at political opponents will use more partisan media than people who are less angry (g path) and they will increase their use of partisan media over time (c path).
4. People who are angry at political opponents will become more politically misinformed over time (d path) and will be more misinformed than people who are less angry (h path).
5. People who are misinformed about politics will use more partisan media over time (e path) and will use more partisan media than people who are more accurately informed (i path).
6. People who are misinformed about politics will become more angry at the outlets' political opponents over time (f path) and will be more angry than people who are more accurately informed (h path).

The model suggests that angry and misinformed individuals will seek out partisan media again in the future. At the same time, this use of partisan media will only serve to strengthen and enhance both anger and false beliefs over time (Slater et al., 2020). In this way, all three concepts – partisan media use, political anger, and political misperceptions – serve as both a cause and effect of each other, reinforcing and strengthening each other over time.

3 Use of Partisan Media

We know that most people are not in media echo chambers but are exposed to partisan media from time to time. This raises several important questions about who uses partisan media, how often, and which outlets are most popular. Before examining the effects of partisan media, it is vital to first understand its prevalence and scope. This section addresses these questions by examining use of partisan media relative to nonpartisan news outlets during the 2020 US election. The analyses in this section lay the groundwork for later questions about the influence of partisan media on anger and misperceptions by offering a descriptive picture of partisan media use during the election.

3.1 Measuring Use of Partisan Media

To examine the frequency of partisan media use, as well as the specific outlets people use, I utilize three waves of survey data (YouGov) collected during the 2020 US election.[2] I began by creating a list of nearly sixty prominent political news outlets, including a mix of partisan and nonpartisan sources. These included a mix of web-only sources (e.g. *Breitbart*, *Slate*), as well as outlets that have both an online and offline presence (e.g. *Fox News*, *ABC News*, *Wall Street Journal*). The list also included both legacy media (e.g. *The New York Times*) and highly partisan sources (e.g. *One American News Network: OANN*). As described later and in the Appendix, each source was then categorized into one of three groups: (1) nonpartisan media (twenty-four sources), (2) liberal partisan media (nineteen sources), and (3) conservative partisan media (sixteen sources).

In each wave of the survey, respondents were presented with the entire list of online sources and asked to select any sources they had used at least once in the past fourteen days for news or political information. Respondents only selected the sources they had used and did not need to respond or check 'no' for unused sources.[3]

While the total number of outlets visited by type provides useful descriptive information, they do not account for frequency of use. Theoretically, an individual who uses an outlet multiple times in a set period of time is likely to be more influenced by content from that outlet than a different individual who uses the site more sparingly. A measure of frequency is therefore needed. After completing the entire battery of source questions, respondents who noted that they had used a specific source were then asked how often they used that source. If, for example, a respondent said they only used *Fox News* in the prior two weeks, they were only asked about their frequency of *Fox News* use. People who used more than one source were then asked about frequency of use for each individual source. To create frequency of use variables, I first took the average frequency for all outlets, by type (nonpartisan, liberal, conservative). Sources within type that were not used were coded as 1 (Never). Average frequencies therefore ranged from 1 (Never) to 7 (Several Times per Day). Individuals who reported not using any sources within type (e.g. conservative media) were coded

---

[2] Complete details about the survey and sample are found in the Appendix.
[3] This approach does not distinguish between active and passive exposure to these sites, as the questionnaire did not ask about whether respondents sought out the source (i.e. selective exposure) or stumbled upon the site incidentally.

as a 1 (Never). This approach allows me to examine discrete exposure to each source (exposed to/not exposed to) as well as the frequency of that use at three time points during the election.

3.2 Categorizing Liberal, Nonpartisan, and Conservative Media

With both the list of outlets and their frequency of use measured, I next needed to categorize sites as liberal, conservative, or nonpartisan. Recall that I earlier noted two defining features of partisan media: partisan media are outlets that (1) cover political issues in a way that is explicitly favorable to one party over the other, and/or (2) are highly critical – often unfairly – of political opponent (Baum & Groeling, 2008). Outlets that do not consistently exhibit these characteristics are defined as nonpartisan. While some outlets are fairly easy to categorize, distinguishing between partisan and nonpartisan sources is at times difficult. There is not a well-established, universally agreed upon list of partisan and nonpartisan sources. As previous authors have noted, any operationalization of what is considered conservative or liberal partisan content is to some extent arbitrary and different categorizations of sources could produce different conclusions (Muise et al., 2022). Further, different researchers may have reasonable and legitimate disagreements about which sources fall into which categories.

Given the challenges inherent in identifying partisan outlets, categorizing sources requires a delicate mix of objective and subjective approaches. I started by comparing existing empirical categorizations of partisan sites based on Twitter sharing behavior (and not actual content) (e.g. Eady et al., 2020) with those from popular websites like AllSides. In most instances, there was consistency in the categorization of sites between these various sources. In the cases of more extreme outlets, the sites were fairly easily characterized as liberal or conservative. However, in some cases categorization was more difficult. Some sources often lean to the left (e.g. *The New York Times*) or right (e.g. the *Wall Street Journal*) in their editorial content without being explicitly partisan in their overall coverage. It is important to note that I am interested in the influence of more directly partisan sites rather than those that at times lean more liberal or conservative. Thus, sources that lean left or right in their editorial coverage but offer fairly nonpartisan news were treated as nonpartisan sites. Nearly all of the sources that were categorized as nonpartisan were those that either do original reporting following traditional journalistic processes, are news aggregators, or are fact-checking sites. In the small number of cases where initial categorization of the source based on prior work was not clear, I visited the sources and made categorization decisions based on my reading of the content and reputation of the source. Although this strategy does rely in part on some subjective assessments, the resulting categorizations offer strong face validity. For example, well-known liberal outlets like *Daily Kos* and *HuffPost* are classified as partisan outlets on the left, while prominent sites like *Fox News* and *Breitbart* are categorized as conservative media outlets. While the approach used has many strengths, it is important to acknowledge that in some cases an argument could be made that a site fits better in a different category.

Some of the more difficult cases to categorize exist at the line between nonpartisan and liberal sources. The conservative media ecosystem is a more cohesive and closed network of sources that are similar in content and tone, without an exact equivalent on the left (Benkler et al., 2018). Conservative partisan media tend to use anger and outrage as a narrative structure and are often more direct in showing their political positions than liberal media (Young, 2019). Establishing liberal media was therefore more difficult. For example, some liberal-leaning sources tend to cover politics in a more entertainment-driven format (e.g. *Buzzfeed*) or offer explainers and commentary on politics (e.g. *Vox*). While these outlets may be somewhat less explicit in their political leanings than some more prominent conservative outlets, I categorized them (and other similar outlets) as liberal in part because of audience perceptions of the sources. Sources that are perceived by the public as alternative (partisan) should not be considered mainstream news (Holt et al., 2019). For several of the liberal sources, my classifications relied in part on data from *Pew* showing that Democrats and liberals are more likely to use and trust sites like *Buzzfeed* or *Vox* than are conservatives (Pew, 2020).

The most challenging categorization was for *CNN*. *CNN* was one of the top-two most popular news sources among survey respondents, with nearly 40% of the sample having used *CNN* in each wave. The question is whether to categorize *CNN* as liberal (i.e. partisan) media or a nonpartisan source. One concern centers on whether people perceive *CNN* to be a partisan site. Most people likely know that they will see explicitly partisan content when they visit certain partisan sites like *Breitbart* or *Mother Jones*, but do *CNN* consumers expect liberal content? Prior research has found that Democrats prefer news from *CNN* over other sources and that Republicans tend to avoid *CNN* as a source for news (Iyengar & Hahn, 2009). A recent Pew survey found that *CNN* was the most trusted news source for Democrats (67% trust it) and the most *distrusted* news source for Republicans (58% distrust it) (Pew, 2020). Additionally, *CNN* was frequently the target of accusations of media bias and fake news from Republican politicians' – including President Trump. All of this suggests that many Americans see *CNN* as more liberal than neutral. Further, content analyses during the 2020 election show that six of the ten most covered stories during the election were criticisms of Donald Trump (Broockman & Kalla, 2023). While criticism of a politician is not inherently biased or partisan, many media critics speculate that *CNN's* abundant negative coverage of Trump was a calculated effort to build an audience and boost ratings (Smith, 2020). Given the nature of *CNN's* political coverage in 2020, the polarization surrounding *CNN* and audiences' perceptions of political bias, I categorized *CNN* as left-leaning partisan outlet.

3.3 How Often Do People Use Partisan Media and What Outlets Do They Use?

Before describing use of partisan media, I begin with some observations about news use in general. Across all fifty-nine news sites – including nonpartisan, conservative, and liberal sources, people on average reported using between seven and eight sources in each wave. In Wave 1, 7.2% of respondents used none of these news sources and 23% used two or less. As seen in Figure 2, the modal response was four sources (out of fifty-nine). The long-tail distribution indicates that the majority of people used just a few sources, while a small number of individuals are exposed to a significant number of sources.

Figure 3 displays the number of nonpartisan sources used by survey respondents in Wave 1. The most common number of sources used was 0, with 18.4% of the sample not using a single nonpartisan source and a majority of people (50.1%) used three or less sources. On average, across all 24 nonpartisan sources, people used 4.69 of the sources in Wave 1, 4.48 in Wave 2, and 4.22 in Wave 3. If I look at frequency of use rather than number of sites used, the data

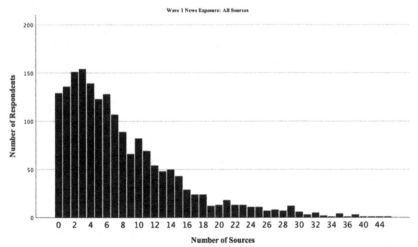

Figure 2 Number of sources used in Wave 1: All sources.

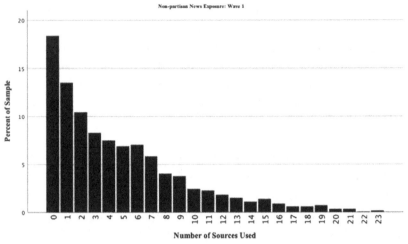

Figure 3 Number of sources used in Wave 1: Nonpartisan sources.

suggest that people who visited news sites did so somewhat infrequently, typically between once and a few times per week in each wave.

The data presented in Figures 4–6 illustrate the percent of the sample exposed to content from each type of source in each wave. These exposure patterns highlight a few important trends. Notably, a few nonpartisan sources were relatively popular, with *The New York Times*, *NBC News*, *The Washington Post*, *Google News*, *ABC News*, *CBS News*, and *NPR* being used at least once in the previous two weeks by approximately 25–30% of the sample. Several other nonpartisan outlets reached between 10 and 25% of the sample.

Use of nonpartisan news during the election was somewhat modest but what about use of partisan media? The trend with the partisan outlets was different. Unsurprisingly, people used partisan sources less frequently than nonpartisan sources; most people who visited partisan media used them sparingly. On average, respondents in each wave visited less than two (1.7) out of the nineteen liberal sources measured and a little more than one (1.3) out of the sixteen conservative sources. Overall, 41.9% of people never visited a liberal source in Wave 1 and 46.7% visited *zero* conservative sources in the first wave (18.4% did not use a nonpartisan source). Only one liberal (*CNN*) and conservative (*Fox News*) outlet surpassed the 30% threshold and nearly all of the remaining partisan outlets failed to reach 10% of the sample in each wave. The data suggest a long-tail distribution of partisan media use; people may occasionally see content from a few prominent sources but the majority of partisan sources receive relatively little attention. Partisan media were not widely or frequently used by most people in the survey.

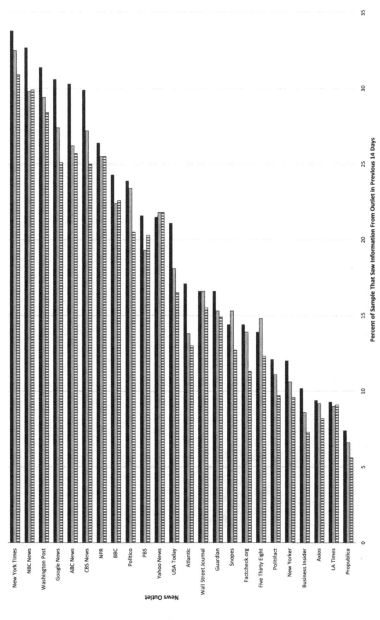

Figure 4 Percent of sample exposed to nonpartisan news outlets by wave.

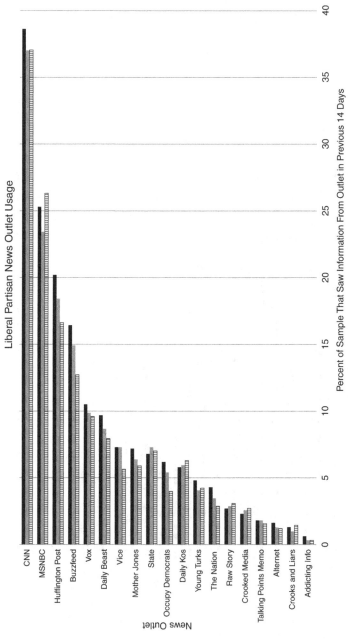

Figure 5 Percent of sample exposed to liberal partisan outlets by wave.

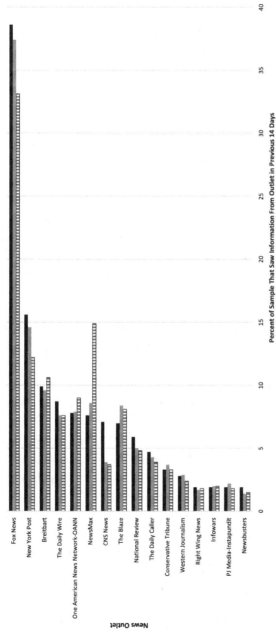

Figure 6 Percent of sample exposed to conservative partisan outlets by wave.

Notably, many partisan sources were used by less than 5% of the sample in Wave 1 (which translates to less than 90 people out of 1,800). More hyper-partisan sites like *Mother Jones, Occupy Democrats, Daily Kos,* and *Young Turks* on the left and *Breitbart, OANN,* and *Daily Caller* on the right had relatively meager audiences. While these audience sizes are very consistent with prior research using both web-tracking (Guess, 2021; Weeks et al., 2023; Wojcieszak et al., 2023) and survey measures (e.g. Fletcher et al., 2021), they do stand in contrast to popular narratives about large partisan media audiences. The overwhelming majority of people do not use hyper-partisan news sources online.

That said, *CNN* and *Fox News* had the highest percent of respondents who indicated they used the sources at least once. This suggests that if people did see content from a liberal or conservative source, in many cases it came from one of these two sources. To test this, I looked at the percentage of users of liberal and conservative media who used *only CNN* or *Fox News*, respectively. 20.7% of users of liberal media only used *CNN*, while 26% of users of conservative media turned to *Fox News* but not any other conservative sources. This is not surprising given the ubiquity and brand recognition of *CNN* and *Fox News*. In addition, these numbers closely reflect Pew (2020) polls showing that *CNN* is the most trusted political news source among Democrats in the United States, while *Fox News* is the most trusted news sources among Republicans.

While use of partisan media was low, many critics argue that the internet allows individuals to create like-minded echo chambers (Bennett & Iyengar, 2008; Sunstein, 2007). Although there is little evidence of partisan echo chambers in the United States (see Fletcher et al., 2021), there remains a possibility that some small segments of the population are isolating themselves only to like-minded partisan media sources while ignoring other sources that could provide information they disagree with (González-Bailón et al., 2023; Jamieson et al., 2023).

To test for echo chambers, I looked for the number of respondents who *only* used liberal or conservative sources, while ignoring nonpartisan sources and partisan sources that support an opposing ideology or party. Using data from Wave 1, I first looked for conservative media echo chambers. To be considered a conservative media echo chamber, a respondent had to have visited at least one of the sixteen conservative media sites but did not use other sources that are nonpartisan or liberal. In total, only 8.5% of the sample visited at least one conservative news site but did not use nonpartisan news or liberal partisan media. This directly contradicts popular claims about widespread audience isolation and echo chambers. Rather, most users of conservative media also see other political information sources. In fact, 81.5% of users of conservative media also used at least one nonpartisan source, and 55.2% visited at least one liberal media source.

I next looked at liberal echo chambers, using the same approach. Liberal sources were used even less exclusively than conservative ones. Only 1.3% of the entire sample used at least one liberal source but no nonpartisan or conservative sources. Among users of liberal media, 95.6% also used a nonpartisan source and 50.7% used a conservative source. The overwhelming majority of those using partisan media at least occasionally use nonpartisan sources and nearly half of those using partisan media also used media sources that offer an opposing ideological perspective. It is important to note that the percentage of people who used no news at all (7.2%) is roughly comparable to the number of people in conservative echo chambers and greater than those in liberal echo chambers. Taken together, the data allow me to conclude that very few people are isolating themselves to partisan media echo chambers online. Rather, the majority of people get at least some news from a variety of different sources.

To this point I have only looked at the number of partisan sources used and not frequency of use. Looking only at the number of sources used may mask the types of audiences drawn to partisan media. It may be that some users of partisan media don't use a lot of sources but rather turn to a small number of outlets quite often. In this case, audiences for partisan media may be selective but loyal. To test this possibility, I also looked beyond a dichotomous use/don't use measure to assess whether frequency of partisan media use changes the story about exposure to these sources.

A similar trend is evident when looking at frequency of use. Those who used partisan media during the election campaign, tended to use those partisan outlets less frequently than they did nonpartisan ones. In each wave, the mean frequency of use for the nonpartisan outlets fell between three and four on the 7-point scale, which reflects using the source between once and a few times per week. In contrast, the average frequency of use for both liberal and conservative partisan media was between once in the prior fourteen days and once per week (between 2 and 3 on the 7-point scale).

3.4 Who Uses Partisan Media and Why?

Most people do not use partisan media often and, if they do, they also tend to use other sources of news and information as well. But some people clearly do rely on partisan media for political information. Before testing the effects of partisan media, it is first important to understand who uses these sources and why. An abundance of evidence shows that strong partisans and ideologues are drawn to like-minded partisan media, often because it provides them political content that reinforces their existing attitudes and beliefs (e.g. Levendusky, 2013; Stroud, 2011). So we would expect that stronger Republicans and conservatives are drawn to conservative media, while stronger Democrats and liberals are more likely to opt for liberal media sources. While partisanship and ideology certainly have roles in attracting audiences to partisan media, other factors like (dis)trust in news can drive people to use partisan sources; people who distrust mainstream news or find it biased are also likely drawn to partisan news (Hmielowski et al., 2022; Holt et al., 2019).

To examine who uses partisan news and why, I used the 2020 survey data to run a series of ordinary least squares (OLS) regressions predicting frequency of conservative and liberal media use (using the same categories described earlier) during the election (see Table A.1). These models look only at use in Wave 1 and therefore are not able to make a causal argument for why people use partisan media. They also do not capture whether people actively selected these media or were incidentally exposed. But they do offer a snapshot into who is using partisan media – including the demographics of users – and what may draw them to those sites. For comparison, I also ran a model that predicted frequency of use of nonpartisan news in the first wave.

Unsurprisingly, conservative people use more conservative online sources and liberal people use more liberal sources. But there are hints that audiences of conservative sources are dedicated, highly active partisans who are engaged in politics in a way that audiences for liberal media are not. People who use conservative media online are very interested in politics, exhibit a lot of distrust in more mainstream media outlets, and are very engaged in politics and political expression online. Audiences for conservative partisan media are more likely to see political content on social media and are more likely to express their political views on these platforms as well. This is somewhat different from audiences of liberal media, who are interested and express themselves politically on social media but do not distrust mainstream sources and are less likely to use social media for political purposes. It is also interesting to note that use of nonpartisan, conservative, and liberal media were all associated with each other. This lends additional support to the notion that audiences are not entirely segregated or siloed and in fact exhibit a reasonable degree of overlap. Rather than viewing partisan content in isolation, it seems that partisan media users on both the left and the right tend to also be at least occasionally interested in nonpartisan news and political content from the other side as well.

What is perhaps most surprising is that party identification does not strongly predict use of either conservative or liberal media. In other words, partisanship – identifying as a strong Republican or Democratic – does not necessarily increase the likelihood that people will use partisan news. Why might this be the case? First, simply being a Republican or Democrat does not inherently mean that someone is going to use partisan sites; partisan identification alone may not be enough to draw people to these sites. Rather, there is evidence that in some cases anger is more influential than partisanship for media choice. Second, the data also suggest that ideology might offer a better explanation than party identification for partisan media use. It is difficult to pinpoint why this is the case. It may be that partisan media sites speak to people's ideological principles rather than partisan ones. Take the case of conservative partisan media. It was at times critical of mainstream Republicans (e.g. calling them RINOs (Republican In Name Only) during and after the Trump presidency and such criticisms may have turned off many Republicans but attracted more conservative users. Regardless of why, ideology seems to push people to partisan sources more than partisanship.

If party identification does not predict partisan media use, what else could explain why people use these sources? Anger may be the key to understanding partisan media use. I argue that partisan media make their audiences angry but also that angry people tune into partisan media. The regression models from the 2020 data show that is clearly the case, at least for conservative media. As seen in Figures 7 and 8, the angrier people are at Joe Biden, the more likely they are to use conservative media. The same pattern is not evident with liberal media – people who were more angry at Donald Trump were no more likely to use liberal media sources than people less angry at Trump. Rather, more anger at

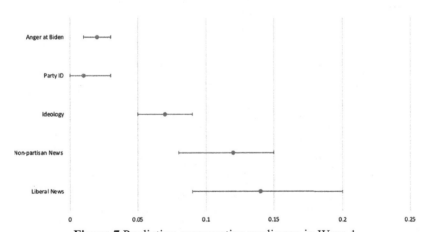

Figure 7 Predicting conservative media use in Wave 1

Note. X axis indicates unstandardized regression coefficients. Regression models control for several variables not shown in the figure including political interest, political knowledge, distrust of mainstream media, social media use for political information, political expression on social media, age, gender, education, and race. See Table A.1 for all coefficients.

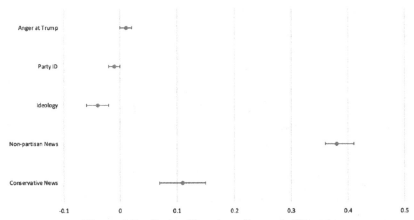

Figure 8 Predicting liberal media use in Wave 1.

Note. X axis indicates unstandardized regression coefficients. Regression models control for several variables not shown in the figure including political interest, political knowledge, distrust of mainstream media, social media use for political information, political expression on social media, age, gender, education, and race. See Table A.1 for all coefficients.

Trump was associated with more *nonpartisan* media use. Thus, the first instance of asymmetry in effects between conservative and liberal media emerges; conservative media audiences tend to be drawn to these outlets by anger at Biden, but anger at Trump is not a strong predictor of liberal media use (at least cross-sectionally).

A few conclusions can be drawn from these analyses on partisan media use. First, while ideology is predictive of liberal media use, there appears to be considerably overlap in liberal and nonpartisan news audiences. Second, it is striking that partisanship did not predict partisan media use. This suggests that other factors – like ideology, credibility, and anger – may be quite influential in driving audiences to partisan news. Finally, the data suggest that those who use partisan media may have different characteristics depending on whether they tend to use conservative or liberal sources. Notably audiences for conservative news are somewhat different than audiences for nonpartisan or liberal media, as they were highly interested in politics, more engaged with political content on social media, and more angry than audiences of other types of news. This is consistent with other work showing that conservative partisan news pages on Facebook tend to get more likes, comments, and shares than mainstream or liberal sources (Hiaeschutter-Rice & Weeks, 2021). So while conservative news audiences remain small, these initial analyses provide evidence that they are different from other media consumers.

4 Political Anger

The United States has become increasingly polarized over the past several decades and much of that polarization is affective or emotional. Partisans increasingly dislike members of the opposing political party and use negative, emotionally charged language to describe opponents (Iyengar et al., 2019). These negative feelings often extend to political leaders, as people have become angrier at elected official and those running for office. Anger has also become a campaign strategy, as many candidates for national office use anger-inducing rhetoric about political opponents to try to gin up electoral support and mobilize political action (Webster, 2020). The rise of anger in electoral politics in America raises a number of important questions: how angry were people at the two major presidential candidates – Donald Trump and Joe Biden? To what extent did partisan media exposure trigger those feelings of anger? And is anger related to false beliefs about politics?

4.1 How Angry Were People at the Presidential Candidates in 2020?

To understand the relationships between partisan media use, anger, and misperceptions, it is first necessary to gauge how angry people were during the campaign. To do so, I asked people in each wave of the survey how angry and mad they were at both Biden and Trump. Mean levels of anger toward each candidate in each wave is plotted in Figures 9 and 10. The Figures illustrate a couple of important trends in political anger. First, as seen in Figure 9, across all respondents there was significantly more anger directed toward Trump than Biden. For example, in the first wave anger at Trump (M = 4.02, SD = 2.64) was

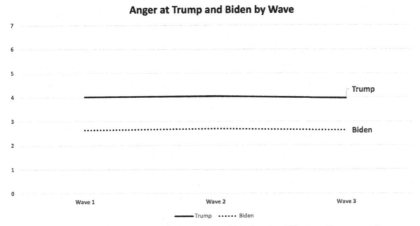

Figure 9 Mean anger toward Trump and Biden by Wave, all respondents.

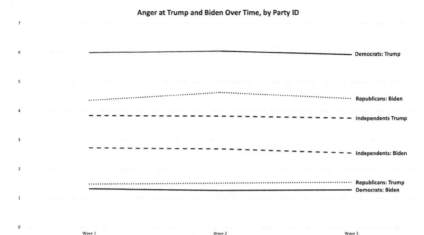

Figure 10 Mean anger toward Trump and Biden by Party ID and Wave.

almost a point and a half higher on the seven-point scale than was anger directed at Biden (M = 2.63, SD = 2.16). This pattern was evident in Waves 2 and 3 as well. Second, mean levels of anger directed toward both candidates were consistent (i.e. flat) across all three waves, which suggests that at a group level mean scores of anger did not vary or change much during the campaign. People, on average, were no more or less angry at Trump or Biden at the end of the campaign compared to the beginning. This may be in part due to people having established feelings about the candidates, both of whom had been prominent national figures prior to the election. And third, as we would expect, respondents expressed considerably more anger at the opposing party's candidate than they did at their own candidates. For example, Democrats' mean level of anger at Trump was near a 6 on the 7-point scale in each wave, while anger at Biden fell between 1 and 2. A similar trend is evident with Republicans, though Republicans were on average less angry with Biden than Democrats were with Trump. Averages for in-party anger suggest that people simply do not express much anger at their party's candidate in the aggregate. I also looked at Independents' anger toward both candidates and found that these nonpartisans were more angry at Trump than they were at Biden in all three waves of the survey.

4.2 What Predicts Political Anger?

Clearly people were angry with the presidential candidates in 2020. Such anger predictably fell along partisan lines as well, as people tended to be considerably more angry at the candidate from the opposing party than they were at their own

Anger at Trump and Biden by Media Sources Used

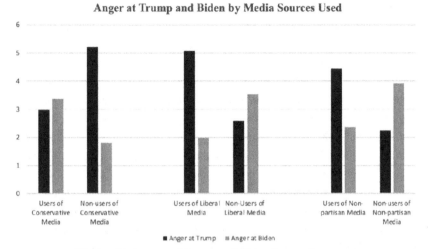

Figure 11 Anger at Trump and Biden by media source

candidate. This suggests that partisanship certainly drives feelings of anger at political candidates. But what else predicts anger? I argue that partisan media also promote political anger. That is, audiences of conservative partisan media should be more angry at Biden than those who infrequently or do not consume conservative media and audiences of liberal partisan media outlets should be more angry at Trump.

Figure 11 demonstrates the mean levels of anger at Trump and Biden for users and nonusers of different types of media. Users of conservative, liberal, or nonpartisan outlets were those who reported using at least one of these respective sources in the first wave of the survey. It is important to note that these categories are not mutually exclusive. For example, the bar representing users of conservative media includes people who visited one conservative site in Wave 1 but the majority of those users also used at least one nonpartisan source and many used a liberal source as well. Those users of conservative sources who also use other types of sources are accounted for in these analyses. This approach therefore does not assume that people who use one type of media (e.g. conservative partisan media) are ignoring other types of media (e.g. nonpartisan).

A few patterns stand out in Figure 11. There is evidence that anger directed at Trump and Biden varies by the media sources people use. Users of Conservative media were more angry at Biden than were nonusers, while users of liberal and nonpartisan sources were angrier at Trump than nonusers. Users of partisan media were also less angry at the outlet-aligned candidate, as users of conservative partisan media were less angry at Trump than nonusers and users of liberal media were less angry at Biden than nonusers. Clearly audiences of these various sources experienced different levels of anger directed toward the two presidential candidates.

To more formally test the influence of partisan media use on political anger, I ran a pair of OLS regressions predicting anger at Biden and Trump in Wave 1. I included a series of demographic and political variables in the models to account for other explanations for political anger. Again, these cross-sectional models cannot conclusively demonstrate what causes political anger but do provide some insights into what is associated with anger. As evident in Figure 10, party ID is a major factor in political anger. Democrats are far angrier than Republicans at Trump and Republicans are angrier at Biden than are Democrats.

Partisan media also play a vital role in anger, at least for conservative media. As the frequency of conservative media use increases, so too does anger at Biden. This suggests that the more people used conservative media, the more angry they were at Biden. Figure 11 takes a closer look at this relationship by plotting levels of anger at Biden by conservative media use. When people do not use conservative media, they do not exhibit much anger at Biden. However, anger at Biden is considerable among users of conservative media. Figure 12 plots the coefficients from the regression predicting anger at Joe Biden and shows that use of conservative media is a powerful driver of anger at Biden. In fact, conservative media is just as influential in eliciting anger at Biden as is Party ID (see Figure 12).

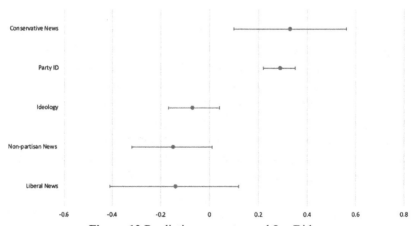

Figure 12 Predicting anger toward Joe Biden.
Note. X axis indicates unstandardized regression coefficients. Regression models control for several variables not shown in the figure including political interest, political knowledge, distrust of mainstream media, social media use for political information, political expression on social media, age, gender, education, and race. See Table A.2 for all coefficients.

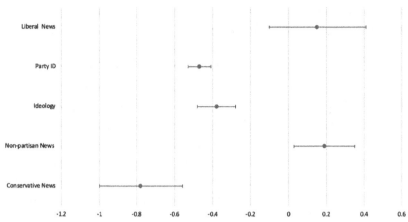

Figure 13 Predicting anger toward Donald Trump.

Note. X axis indicates unstandardized regression coefficients. Note that higher values for Party ID and Ideology represent stronger Republican and conservative identification, respectively. Regression models control for several variables not shown in the figure including political interest, political knowledge, distrust of mainstream media, social media use for political information, political expression on social media, age, gender, education, and race. See Table A.2 for all coefficients.

The same pattern is not found with use of liberal media. Once again, this offers evidence of asymmetry in effects between conservative and liberal media. Frequency of liberal media use is not associated with anger at Trump (see that confidence interval crosses zero in Figure 13). There are a few possible explanations for this lack of a relationship between liberal media use and anger. First, anger at Trump was considerable and being both a Democrat and liberal explained much of the anger at Trump (as indicated by the negative coefficients – Democratic or liberal identification were on the low end of the scales). It may be that using liberal partisan media has little added ability to explain anger at Trump above and beyond party identification and ideology. Second, it seems anger directed at Trump is associated with use of nonpartisan media. This is not surprising given that nonpartisan news outlets devoted heavy coverage to the various scandals facing Trump during his presidency. Given the significant overlap in audience for nonpartisan and liberal media, it may be that the relatively low levels of liberal partisan media use are not enough to make people angrier at Trump, over and above the influence of nonpartisan media. A final possibility for the discrepancy in the influence of conservative and liberal media on political anger may stem from different content in these various outlets. Conservative media purposefully uses anger to draw audiences (Berry & Sobieraj, 2013; Young, 2019) and the data here indicate that it is successful in eliciting anger in users in a way that liberal partisan media typically do not.

5 Effects of Partisan Media and Anger on Political Misperceptions

The evidence reported here and elsewhere illustrates that most Americans do not exist in partisan media echo chambers but rather have media diets that are more balanced in terms of the types of sources they use – if they use news at all (roughly 7% of people used no news). But this does not mean that partisan media are not influential in shaping the attitudes, feelings, and beliefs of those who are exposed to these sources. As demonstrated in the previous section, audiences of conservative media outlets exhibit more anger toward Joe Biden than do people who do not frequently use conservative media. There may be other effects of partisan media as well. By covering political scandals, rumors, conspiracy theories, and other unsubstantiated claims, or by ignoring negative information about their preferred party, partisan media may be misinforming their audience and contributing to public beliefs that are not factually accurate. There is some evidence that this is in fact happening. Users of partisan media have been shown to be more accepting of political falsehoods if they are politically beneficial to their preferred party. For instance, users of conservative media were more likely to believe false claims that reflected poorly on the Democratic party/politicians or liberals, and, in some cases, audiences of liberal partisan media were more accepting of misinformation that would reflect negatively on Republicans or conservatives (e.g. Feldman et al., 2014; Garrett et al., 2016; Weeks et al., 2023).

The association between use of partisan media and holding misperceptions leaves open several questions. First, it is difficult to determine if partisan media *cause* political misperceptions. Surveys that measure media use and false beliefs at only one period of time cannot establish causality, as it is difficult to establish whether use of partisan media leads to false beliefs or whether those with false beliefs are drawn to partisan media. Second, the existence of a relationship between partisan media and false beliefs does not illustrate *how* or *why* those beliefs emerge; we know the process of belief formation is not as simple as people merely believing every bit of information that partisan media might provide. It is therefore necessary to understand the process through which partisan media impact beliefs. This chapter uses multi-wave survey data to examine the relationship between partisan media use and misperceptions over time. Doing so allows for a stronger examination of the question of causality and provides a more informed answer to the question of whether partisan media cause false beliefs and, if so, how. My expectation is that partisan media make people angry at political opponents, which in turn makes them more likely to believe false claims about those opponents.

In the following sections, I unpack this relationship in several ways. I first look at the degree to which partisan media and anger are predictive of political misperceptions at the start of the campaign. Next, I take advantage of the time component of the data to better unpack the causal nature of the relationships between partisan media, anger, and misperceptions over the course of the election. Although I report on how partisan media and anger shape several different false beliefs in 2020, I will focus on and emphasize a few prominent claims to illustrate the nature of these relationships.

5.1 Do People Believe False Claims about Politics?

In each of the three waves of the 2020 YouGov survey, I asked respondents to report the extent to which they believed a series of political, scientific, and health statements to be true or false. All but one of the statements were false. Following definitions of misinformation, determination of truth was made based on the best available evidence from relevant experts at the time the study was conducted (Vraga & Bode, 2020). In some cases, the statements were aligned with or benefitted the Republican party, politicians, or viewpoints (and presumably more likely to be believed by Republicans), while others favored Democratic party members, politicians, or views. Several of the claims were targeted at the two major presidential candidates in 2020 (Trump and Biden). Some claims were about the presidential candidates' health or personality, some were about policies they supported, while others focused on scandals or conspiracy theories.

The claims selected represent some of the most prominent forms of misinformation and conspiracy theories that were circulating in the United States the fall of 2020. However, it is important to note that the claims are not representative of the population of misperceptions held by Americans in 2020. There is also ideological asymmetry in the claims, as many of the statements that favor conservatives (e.g. election integrity, claims about Biden, Covid) were spread more widely and were better known than those that favor liberals (Harber et al., 2021). Despite these limitations, the claims do provide a reasonable test of the dynamics I have discussed in this Element. Many of the claims were covered extensively by partisan media or spread by prominent elected officials like former President Donald Trump. For example, Joe Biden was often falsely accused of recommending the removal of a Ukrainian prosecutor for the benefit of his son Hunter, while serving as Vice President. Democrat-aligned claims included the falsehood that government agencies had compromising video footage of Donald Trump with prostitutes in a Moscow hotel room. At the time, and to date, there is

Table 1 Claims evaluated

Republican-aligned claims:
1. Joe Biden supports defunding the police (False)
2. While serving as US Vice President, Joe Biden recommended removing a Ukrainian prosecutor for investigating a company connected to his son, Hunter (False)
3. The coronavirus (Covid-19) was intentionally planned, created, and released so that billionaires like Bill Gates can profit from it (False)
4. Joe Biden sexually assaulted a former Senate aid in 1993 (False)
5. Donald Trump is fighting a group of politicians and celebrities who operate a child sex-trafficking ring (False)

Democrat-aligned claims:
1. Donald Trump ordered US Postmaster General Louis DeJoy to slow down mail services to help Trump win the 2020 presidential election (False)
2. Donald Trump sought medical attention for a series of strokes he has had while serving as president (False)
3. The Trump administration attempted to get US medical experts into China to study the coronavirus outbreak in early 2020 (True)
4. The Russian government possesses a video tape of Donald Trump with prostitutes in a Moscow hotel room in 2013 (False)

Other claims (mostly Republican-aligned):
1. Facemasks are an effective measure in slowing the spread of Covid-19 (True)/ Facemasks are not an effective measure in slowing the spread of Covid-19
2. Vaccines are generally safe and effective (True)/Vaccines are risky and harmful
3. There is no evidence of widespread voter fraud in US elections (True)/There is evidence of widespread voter fraud in US elections

---

Note. Determination of whether the claim was true or false was based on best available evidence from relevant experts at the time the study was fielded. For some claims, new evidence may emerge since November 2020 that changes whether it is true or false.

no conclusive evidence to support either of these claims. Some of the claims were more known than others, including false claims spread by Trump and others about election fraud in the US. Examining both well- and lesser-known falsehoods allows me to test whether more prominent claims fit the model better than more obscure ones. All of the claims examined here are listed in Table 1.

Before examining the influence of partisan media and anger on false beliefs, it is first necessary to have a baseline understanding of the degree to which people believed the various pieces of misinformation. Figures 14–16 depict the

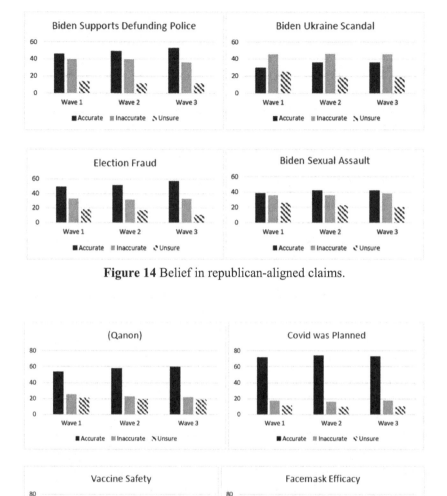

Figure 14 Belief in republican-aligned claims.

Figure 15 Belief in Covid-related claims and Qanon.

percentage of the sample who held accurate beliefs, inaccurate beliefs, or were unsure of the truth for each of the twelve claims in each of the three waves.

A few patterns in the distribution of beliefs stand out. First, none of the claims are outright rejected as false. For example, the claims on which people were most accurate were those related to Covid. Roughly 70% of the sample

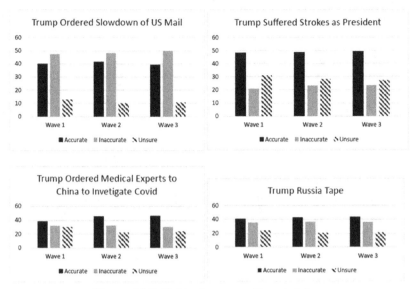

Figure 16 Belief in democrat-aligned claims

accurately believed that Covid was not planned and that masks and vaccines are effective. None of the other claims reached a 60% accuracy threshold, which may in part be because they are more explicitly partisan.

Second, for two of the explicitly partisan claims there were more people who were misinformed than accurately informed, based on the best available evidence. For example, despite no strong evidence that it was true, more than 40% of people said that Joe Biden inappropriately interfered in Ukrainian politics in order to benefit his son, Hunter. Similarly, nearly 50% of people falsely believed that Donald Trump ordered a slowdown of US mail in order to gain an electoral advantage. These two claims were the only ones for which more people were inaccurate than accurate.

However, all of the remainder of the claims were believed by significant percentages of survey respondents. For example, nearly 40% of respondents falsely believed that Joe Biden supported defunding the police and that he had sexually assaulted a Senate aide in the 1990s. Almost 40% of respondents also believed that a tape existed in which Donald Trump was with prostitutes in a Russian hotel room, an unsupported claim that came out of the much-criticized Steele dossier. While this 40% threshold likely represents biased information processing among many partisans, given that approximately 36% of respondents were Democrats and 25% were Republicans, these levels of false belief indicate that many Independents are also misinformed and that some partisans accept false claims that reflect poorly on their own party. The belief levels also indicate a great deal of uncertainty about what people think is true. In many cases, the unsure responses hovered around 20%.

While misperceptions were slightly higher for many of the Republican-aligned claims about Biden than were the Democratic-aligned claims about Trump, the differences were not drastic. Despite not receiving the same level of news coverage or discussion on social media, many of the more obscure Democratic-aligned claims (e.g. Trump suffered strokes while President) were believed by between one-fifth to one-third of the sample. Although the Republican-aligned claims certainly received more attention during the election, it is not the case that such claims are the only ones believed.

The extent to which people believed two prominent claims about election fraud and Qanon are important and interesting to note. False claims about election fraud were likely some of the most shared during the election and were propagated by Trump and many of his supporters. Roughly half of the sample correctly said widespread election fraud does not occur in US elections, but the other half of respondents believed that it did or were unsure if it did. Again, the percentage of misinformed individuals on this particular claim far exceeds the number of Republicans in the sample, meaning that many Independents and perhaps even some Democrats are misinformed or have doubts about the integrity of US elections. Perhaps the most surprising result when looking at belief levels is the fact that more than 20% of people believed the conspiracy theory that Donald Trump was secretly fighting a group of Democrats who were running a sex trafficking operation.[4] This is one of the core tenets of the Qanon conspiracy theory.

Finally, it is important to note that in the aggregate, beliefs changed very little over time. For nearly all of the claims, the percentage of people who held accurate or inaccurate beliefs or were unsure were very consistent in all three waves. While at the individual level some beliefs changed (as described later), this was not true in the aggregate despite, in many cases, repeated debunking of the claims by journalists and political figures. This suggests that once misinformation is established, it is very difficult to correct at the population level.[5]

---

[4] This finding needs to be taken with a bit of caution and should not be interpreted as Qanon support; the question about Donald Trump secretly fighting a Democratic-led sex trafficking ring does not explicitly tap Qanon endorsement but rather one facet of it. Measuring Qanon support is notoriously difficult and the strongest predictors of Qanon beliefs are conspiratorial worldviews, dark triad beliefs, and support for nonnormative behavior, rather than political ideology (Enders et al., 2022).

[5] There is some debate over whether reported beliefs like these represent true beliefs or other processes such as partisan cheerleading (see Graham, 2023). It could be, for example, that people respond to these survey questions in a way that makes their side look good, particularly if they are angry. For instance, perhaps Republican respondents do not actually believe that Joe Biden supports defunding the police but respond that they do because they are angry at him and it

5.2 Do Partisan Media Cover Political Misinformation?

When looking at the accuracy of people's beliefs about false claims spread during the 2020 US election it is clear that many people were misinformed. In fact, for many of these claims only a minority of people were accurately informed. I argue that partisan media play an important role in misinforming audiences. However, this argument is predicated on the assumption that partisan media actually cover these falsehoods. After all, if partisan media don't cover false claims, they cannot cause people to have false beliefs about those claims. Existing research suggests that they do, as partisan media – particularly conservative sources – often amplify and spread political misinformation online (Vargo et al., 2018; Zhang et al., 2023). For example, during the outbreak of Covid-19 and the subsequent introduction of a vaccine, conservative partisan media spread misinformation about the virus (Motta et al., 2020) introduced Covid-related conspiracy theories (McCann Ramirez, 2022) and reported more anti-vaccine content (Savillo & Monroe, 2021). This coverage of false or misleading information is not new, as conservative partisan media outlets have also historically emphasized unsubstantiated claims about issues like climate change (e.g. Feldman et al., 2012).

Next, I consider the extent to which partisan media cover some of the other false claims included in this project. A comprehensive content analyses of all partisan media coverage – online and on television – of each claim investigated here is beyond the scope of this Element. However, I offer a more limited, selective case study of partisan media coverage of these issues for illustrative purposes. I focus here on two conservative-favored claims (Hunter Biden Ukraine scandal and Joe Biden supports defunding the police) and two liberal ones (Donald Trump ordered the US mail to slowdown for election advantage and Donald Trump suffered strokes while in office). Entering fairly rudimentary search terms (e.g. "Hunter Biden" and "Ukraine") I used Nexis Uni to search for news coverage of these stories between August 1, 2020 and November 3, 2020 (election day). This time window roughly reflects the general election period and also captures coverage from these sources during the time when my survey was in the field. Nexis Uni only reports news coverage from a limited number of outlets but does include coverage from conservative outlets like *Fox News* and the *Daily Caller*, liberal outlets like *CNN* and *MSNBC*, as well as more nonpartisan outlets like the *New York Times*. Of course, these outlets are not

---

makes Republicans look good. This is possible but there are reasons to believe that these beliefs are genuine for most respondents. First, mean levels of belief changed little over the three waves, suggesting they are somewhat stable. Second, the survey included a 'don't know' response option, which lowers the likelihood that people guess or always respond in a partisan way.

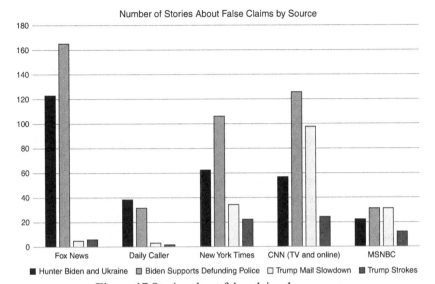

Figure 17 Stories about false claims by source.

Note. The Y-axis indicates total number of reported stories between August 1 and November 3, 2020.

necessarily representative of coverage in the larger partisan media landscape, but they can at least illustrate patterns of the volume of coverage about these claims by various media sources.

These analyses are depicted in Figure 17 and highlight two important patterns: one, partisan media indeed covered stories related to false claims and two, the amount of coverage often reflected the partisan or ideological leaning of the outlet.[6] Looking first at the two conservative/Republican-aligned claims, it is clear that *Fox News* reported more stories on these issues than did liberal or nonpartisan outlets. During the three-month period in late summer and early autumn of 2020, *Fox News* reported approximately 123 stories about Hunter Biden and Ukraine and 165 about the false claim that Biden supported defunding the police. The liberal source *CNN* also reported on these claims (57 and 126 stories, respectively) but the volume of stories was less than *Fox News*. *MSNBC* devoted substantially less coverage, having only twenty-two stories about Hunter Biden and 31 about Biden defunding the police. Interestingly, the

---

[6] Some of the claims do not fit perfectly into ideological patterns. For example, Qanon support is driven more by conspiratorial worldview than ideology or partisanship (Enders et al., 2022). That said, conservative news outlets did in fact cover Qanon during the time period under study. For example, Fox News ran an online story on August 2020 with the headline "Trump praises supporters of Qanon conspiracy theory." This was one of several stories Fox ran on Qanon. Other conservative sites like Breitbart and Daily Caller ran dozens of stories on Qanon during 2020.

conservative online media outlet the *Daily Caller* covered these claims less than both *CNN* and the *New York Times.*

When looking at the liberal-favored claims, we see a very similar pattern with liberal partisan media outlets. *CNN* reported ninety-eight stories about the unsubstantiated claim that Trump ordered a slowdown of the mail and twenty-four stories about Trump suffering strokes while serving as President. These stories also received coverage on the liberal outlet *MSNBC* (thirty-one and twelve stories, respectively) and the *New York Times* (thirty-four and twenty-two). Clearly *CNN* devoted the most coverage to these claims. Although liberal outlets emphasized the stories, they were nearly nonexistent in conservative outlets. *Fox News* ran only five stories about Trump and a mail slowdown and six stories about his alleged strokes. The *Daily Caller* barely covered these stories at all (three and one stories, respectively).

These analyses demonstrate that partisan outlets covered stories related to false claims during the 2020 election, though they are only a limited snapshot into the nature of partisan media coverage of falsehoods. More so, the patterns of coverage emerged in predictable ways, with conservative media outlets devoting attention to conservative-favorable claims and liberal media outlets highlighting liberal-favorable claims. Both conservative and liberal outlets also tended to give less attention to false claims that reflect poorly on their aligned party and candidates. The fairly basic analyses here are limited and only capture coverage of two claims from two partisan outlets from each party. They likely undercount the number of stories from each of these outlets and they also only account for mere mentions of the claims and not the specific details or framing. Even so, the findings suggest partisan media did cover these stories in the lead up to the election. The time period of interest in the analyses was only ninety-four days, meaning that some of these stories were being covered almost twice a day by certain outlets. Scaling that up to reflect all coverage on all partisan outlets suggests that these stories were quite prominent in partisan media ecosystems. Users who turned to these sources frequently were perhaps exposed to dozens, if not hundreds of unsubstantiated claims about these politicians. The next question is whether such coverage influenced beliefs about the false claims.

5.3 Are Partisan Media Audiences More Misinformed?

In the following section, I examine whether partisan media use and political anger promote misperceptions. I start below by looking at mean levels of belief accuracy across those who used liberal and conservative media and those who did not. I then turn to more robust analyses using OLS regression. As noted in

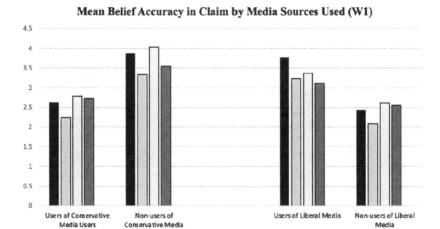

Figure 18 Belief accuracy about Conservative/Republican-aligned claims by partisan media use.

Note. Higher values depict more accurate beliefs.

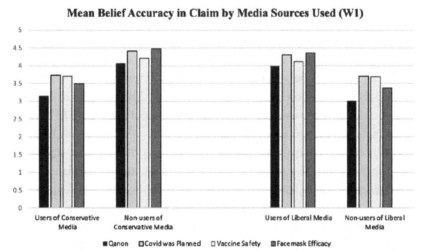

Figure 19 Belief accuracy about Covid-related claims and Qanon by partisan media use.

Note. Higher values depict more accurate beliefs.

the analyses of partisan media and anger, use of liberal partisan media, conservative partisan media, and nonpartisan media are not mutually exclusive. The means reported in Figures 18–20 for use of partisan media include people who also used other types of sources.

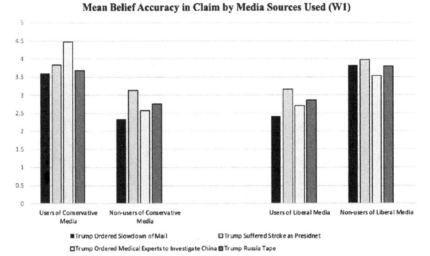

Figure 20 Belief accuracy about Liberal/Democrat-aligned claims
by partisan media use.
Note. Higher values depict more accurate beliefs.

In Figures 18–20, I depict the mean level of belief accuracy in Wave 1 for people who use liberal or conservative media and those who don't. Figure 18 illustrates belief in Conservative/Republican-aligned claims by partisan media use. Recall that taller bars represent more accuracy in assessing the claim and shorter bars indicate more misperceptions. The most interesting point of comparison is that between users of conservative media and nonusers. The bars on the left side of graph clearly indicate that users of conservative media have drastically different beliefs than nonusers; in all cases they are less accurate in assessing the claims. These difference are fairly robust; for all four claims users of conservative media are about a point less accurate on a 5-point scale. Audiences for conservative media do not reach the mid-point of the accuracy scale on any of the claims, with mean belief scores suggesting the typical user reported that each of the four false claims was 'probably true'. This suggests that on average, audiences of conservative partisan media are more inaccurate than accurate in evaluating these statements.

While accuracy improves with the Covid-related claims and Qanon-related statement, users of conservative media remain more misinformed than nonusers for all four of those claims as well (Figure 19). People who do not use conservative media are simply more accurate about these four issues than are users. That said, the average user of conservative media is around the mid-point (3) on the five-point scale for the three Covid-19-related claims, which suggests many users were unsure about the truth. However, the gap between users of conservative media and nonusers is large for the claim about Qanon (about one point on the 5-point scale), suggesting that audiences for conservative media hold considerably less accurate beliefs about this conspiracy theory.

A very similar pattern is evident for liberal media use and belief in Liberal/Democratic-aligned claims. In Figure 20, beliefs of users of liberal media are reported in the cluster second from the right. People who use liberal partisan media are considerably more misinformed about liberal/Democratic aligned claims than their peers who do not use liberal media. For all four claims about Donald Trump, the gap between users of liberal media and nonusers is quite large. For example, the mean level of belief in the claim that Donald Trump deliberately slowed down the US mail is 2.43 for users of liberal media and 3.82 for nonusers. For three out of the four claims, beliefs of users of liberal outlets fall below the mid-point, suggesting on average users were more misinformed than accurately informed. Like audiences of conservative media, audiences of liberal partisan media also believe politically aligned falsehoods at a much greater rate than nonusers.

5.4 Do Partisan Media Use and Political Anger Promote Misperceptions?

Here I consider whether partisan media use and political anger contribute to people's well-documented misperceptions about politics, science, and health. Recall that angry people are more likely to use partisan heuristics when evaluating false claims and are ultimately more likely to be misinformed about attitude-consistent claims (MacKuen et al., 2010; Weeks, 2015). I use OLS regression to predict each of the twelve claims of interest. These models are cross-sectional, meaning that they only look at variables from Wave 1 and do not examine changes in beliefs over time. They should therefore not be interpreted as causal. The models account for numerous demographic and political variables that could also explain political misperceptions, including party ID, ideology, political interest, political knowledge, other types of news use, and trust in media, as well as many others (see Appendix for complete list of variables). By considering these additional variables, I am able to examine the degree to which partisan media use and political anger are uniquely associated with false beliefs. Full regression results for each of the claims are located in the Appendix. In the section following this one, I build on these regressions by presenting a more robust set of analyses that allow me to better test whether partisan media changes anger and belief accuracy over time, providing insights into the causal influence of partisan media.

The initial OLS regressions clearly demonstrate that both use of partisan media and political anger are consistently associated with political misperceptions. Recall that eight of the false claims tend to favor or be consistent with views of conservatives or the Republican party. The other four claims were favorable to liberals and Democrats. For seven out of the eight claims favoring Conservatives/Republicans, the more people used conservative partisan media, the more likely they were to believe the false claims (with beliefs about vaccine safety being the only one not predicted by use of conservative media). In other words, taking into account a number of alternative explanations, people who more frequently used conservative media were more likely to incorrectly believe that election fraud existed, that Joe Biden supported defunding the police, that Donald Trump was fighting a political sex trafficking ring, and that Covid-19 was planned, among other false claims.

The exact same pattern of relationships was found between use of liberal partisan media and the four false claims about Trump. More frequent users of liberal media outlets were more likely to accept as true that Trump ordered a slowdown of the US mail, that he suffered strokes while President, that he did not send Covid investigators to China, and that Russia possessed a comprising tape of him. All together, for eleven out of the twelve claims, using either conservative or liberal partisan media was significantly associated with more outlet-aligned misperceptions about politics, science, and health.

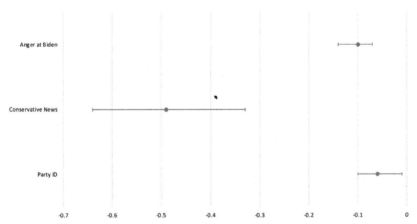

Figure 21 (a) Anger, Conservative Media, and Party ID as Predictors of Misperceptions (Biden Supports Defunding the Police).

Note. Dots represent unstandardized regression coefficients and lines represent 95% confidence intervals. Regression models control for several variables not shown in the figure including political interest, political knowledge, distrust of mainstream media, social media use for political information, political expression on social media, age, gender, education, and race. See Table A.3 for all coefficients.

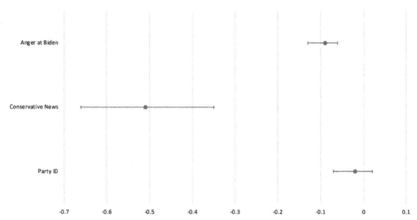

Figures 21 (b) Anger, Conservative Media, and Party ID as Predictors of Misperceptions (Election Fraud).

Note. Dots represent unstandardized regression coefficients and lines represent 95% confidence intervals. Regression models control for several variables not shown in the figure including political interest, political knowledge, distrust of mainstream media, social media use for political information, political expression on social media, age, gender, education, and race. See Table A.3 for all coefficients.

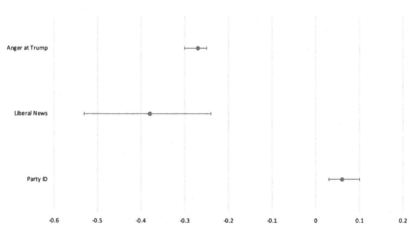

Figure 22 (a). Anger, Liberal Media, and Party ID as Predictors of Misperceptions (Trump Ordered Slowdown of US Mail).

Note. Dots represent unstandardized regression coefficients and lines represent 95% confidence intervals. Regression models control for several variables not shown in the figure including political interest, political knowledge, distrust of mainstream media, social media use for political information, political expression on social media, age, gender, education, and race. See Table A.5 for all coefficients.

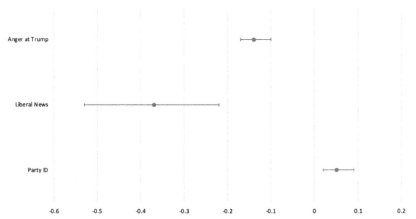

Figure 22 (b). Anger, Liberal Media, and Party ID as Predictors of Misperceptions (Trump Suffered Strokes While President).

Note. Dots represent unstandardized regression coefficients and lines represent 95% confidence intervals. Regression models control for several variables not shown in the figure including political interest, political knowledge, distrust of mainstream media, social media use for political information, political expression on social media, age, gender, education, and race. See Table A.5 for all coefficients.

To illustrate the nature of these relationships, I plot the regression coefficients for partisan media use, anger, and party affiliation in Figures 21 (a, b) and 22 (a, b). The dots in the figures, which represent the relationship (coefficient) between using conservative/liberal media and belief in the false claims, are all less than zero, indicating that the more people used partisan media, the less accurate they were about the claims. In sum, the more people used conservative and liberal media, the more they were misinformed. I only depict the relationship for four of the claims here but the results are very similar across all twelve claims. Similar figures for all of the claims can be found in the Figures A.2a–c, A.3a–c, and A.4a–b of the Appendix.

In addition to use of partisan media, anger was also significantly associated with every one of the twelve misperceptions in predictable ways. When people were angry at Joe Biden, they were more likely to believe the eight false claims that favored conservatives/Republicans. The same was true with use of liberal media, anger at Trump, and false beliefs about Trump. The pattern of consistency is remarkable. Simply put, when people are politically angry at a target (in this case Trump or Biden) they are more likely to hold misperceptions that reflect poorly on that target, including their party or policies.

What is perhaps more striking is that both use of partisan media and political anger are more consistent predictors of political misperceptions than are political party affiliation and political ideology. Party identification and ideology have long been identified as factors that help explain false beliefs. According to the theory of motivated reasoning, people are more likely to believe false claims that reflect well on their worldview or are consistent with prior beliefs (Flynn et al., 2017). In the case of the current analyses, this would suggest that Republicans and conservatives are more likely to believe claims that are favorable to their party or ideology, while Democrats and liberals should be more accepting of falsehoods that favor them. These analyses indicate this is true in some cases but not all. For example, when one accounts for political anger, party affiliation was not significantly associated with false beliefs about the existence of election fraud, that Covid was planned, vaccine safety, or mask efficacy, among others. The influence of ideology on false beliefs was also somewhat inconsistent. What this suggests is that while party and ideology are often important predictors of misperceptions, political anger may play a larger role in shaping beliefs. Being a Republican, for example, may not be enough to believe that election fraud exists but consuming a lot of conservative news or being very angry at Joe Biden seem to tip the scales toward being misinformed. Studies that fail to account for the influence of political anger on beliefs may therefore overstate the effect of partisanship or ideology on misperceptions.

It is important to note that in some cases, using partisan media sites is associated with more accurate beliefs (See Tables A6–8). This tends to occur when the false claims are harmful to a supported candidate or party. For example, people who used more liberal media were more likely to dismiss the three unfavorable claims about Joe Biden, as well as correctly note the lack of evidence of election fraud in US elections. A similar pattern was evident with use of conservative media and negative claims about Trump. In each case, the more people reported using conservative media, the more accurate they were about the negative claims about Trump. This pattern did not hold for claims about vaccine safety, masking, Covid, and Qanon, as audiences of liberal media were no more or less likely to falsely believe those claims.

Yet we consistently find that partisan audiences are quick to dismiss false claims about a political figure or issue that is aligned with the partisan outlet. This set of relationships suggests three possibilities. One, it is very likely that people who are politically predisposed to reject false claims about Biden, for example, are more likely to use liberal media. This is consistent with theories of selective exposure in that Democrats or Biden supporters are more likely to seek out liberal sources with pro-Biden coverage. The same may be true for conservative audiences and conservative sites. The second possibility is that partisan media do not devote much attention to harmful claims about the supported candidate or party. For example, the analyses aforementioned showed that liberal media were less likely to cover harmful claims about Biden than were conservative media. The final possibility is that these partisan sites actively push back on false claims that reflect poorly on aligned candidates or issues. For instance, *Fox New* repeatedly questioned the evidence in the "Steele dossier" that suggested the existence of the so-called 'pee tape' that allegedly depicted Russian prostitutes urinating in front of Trump. In this case, *Fox News* was right to questions these allegations, as no concrete evidence of the tape has since emerged. In this sense, partisan media outlets may facilitate more accurate beliefs by raising doubts and uncertainty about the truth when the false claim in question is targeted at a political figure the outlet supports. This creates the interesting dynamic that partisan media audiences may be more misinformed about political opponents but more accurately informed about supported figures and issues (see Shah et al., 2017).

Finally, much has been said about the value of nonpartisan, centrist media in the fight against misinformation. News that adheres to core journalistic values like truth, accuracy, verification, and fairness are thought to be effective correctives to political falsehoods. Large, national news organizations like *The New York Times* and *The Washington Post* have devoted significant resources to fighting misinformation and adopted catchy slogans to highlight their commitment to truth (*New York Times,* "Truth is Essential: Life Needs Truth"; *Washington Post,* "Democracy Dies in the Darkness").

While noble endeavors, there is mixed evidence in the data here about whether exposure to centrist, nonpartisan news outlets like these improves belief accuracy (See Tables A6–8). For two of the false claims about Joe Biden and the election fraud claim, there is evidence that audiences for nonpartisan news are more accurate in their beliefs about these claims. But the same is not true for three of the four claims about Trump. In these instances, using nonpartisan media had no relationship with beliefs about Trump. Importantly, the same null pattern emerged for nonpartisan news use and beliefs about vaccine safety and the conspiracy theory that Covid-19 was planned. Overall, this suggests that use of nonpartisan media was not associated with more misperceptions, but it also was not consistently associated with more accurate beliefs.

It is promising to see that in some cases, audiences of nonpartisan news were more accurately informed. But this does not hold true across the board. Why? First, it may be that many of these claims are too obscure for nonpartisan news to devote substantial coverage. For example, news organizations are unlikely to run multiple stories about claims that are based on rumors and speculation – and not evidence – that are not widespread. They may devote a single story or two to more outrageous false claims, but generally reporting on such falsehoods or rumors would be inconsistent with the practices of mainstream, objective journalism. Second, information from more mainstream news is very likely subject to biased information processing on the part of both conservatives and liberals. Many conservatives actively distrust mainstream news outlets; only 35% of Republicans have at least some trust in information from national news organizations (Pew, 2021). Given the lack of relationship between use of nonpartisan news and claims about vaccine safety, as well as Covid-19 conspiracy theories, it may be that conservatives exposed to factual information about vaccines and Covid-19 were more skeptical about nonpartisan news coverage because of their distrust. As a result, they were not persuaded by the information. Similarly, nonpartisan news did not improve belief accuracy about Trump. It is possible that audiences' prior beliefs about Trump were strong enough that nonpartisan news coverage rebutting claims about Trump was not enough to facilitate more accurate beliefs.

5.5 Does Partisan Media Use Cause Anger and Political Misperceptions?

The analyses in the previous sections shed important light onto the nature of the relationships between partisan media use, anger, and political misperceptions. They demonstrate that people who consume more partisan media and/or are politically angry are more likely to be misinformed. While informative, such analyses are limited in that they only look at these relationships at one point in time. Such cross-sectional analyses do not allow for any assessment or determination of causality. They do not show, for example, whether use of partisan media causes anger and political misperceptions, or if that anger also causes false beliefs. It is possible that the causal arrow flows in the opposite direction such that people who are angrier or more misinformed are more likely to seek out partisan media. To better tease out the causal influence of these relationships, what is needed is survey data (or experiments) that look at these associations over time. Recall that my survey interviewed the same people at three time periods, or waves, over the course of the 2020 election. This type of panel data allows for more robust tests of causality because it can examine reciprocal relationships between partisan media use, anger, and misperceptions over the election season.

Another benefit of using panel data is that it allows me to distinguish between-person effects from within-person effects, which is important when modeling the effects of exposure to media (Thomas et al., 2021). Between-person effects assess whether patterns of change across time differ across individuals. In this case, I am interested in whether people who use more partisan media experience more anger and are more misinformed over time relative to less frequent users. Within-person effects test whether particular individuals change over time and why. In other words, this approach isolates whether changes in anger or beliefs, for example, are due to or caused by partisan media use. Note that a more detailed description and depiction of the Random Intercept Cross-Lagged Panel Model (RI-CLPM) I use here can be found in the Appendix.

I start by examining between-person associations to assess whether differences in partisan media use can explain differences between individuals in anger and misperceptions over time. For each of the twelve false claims, Tables 2 and 3 report three relationships from the RI-CLPM, including the associations between (1) use of conservative/liberal partisan media and political anger, (2) political anger and belief accuracy, and (3) use of conservative/liberal partisan media and belief accuracy.

Remarkably, the pattern of results is the same across all twelve false claims. The claims were diverse; some targeted Trump, others Biden, some were focused on personality while others policy, and finally, some were rather obscure and extreme. Despite these differences in the nature of the claims, partisan media played a critical role in angering and misinforming audiences. First, significant between-person relationships were found between use of conservative media and anger at Biden and use of liberal media and anger at Trump. This indicates that people who more frequently use partisan media were more angry at the presidential candidate that is opposed by those partisan sources. Second, consistent with my prior research (Weeks, 2015), I find that people who are angry at a political candidate hold fewer accurate beliefs about that candidate or their related policies. People who were angry at Joe Biden were more likely to believe in the existence of voter fraud, as well as various false claims about Biden. This anger also spilled over into beliefs about health, as people who were angry with Biden were also more misinformed about mask efficacy and vaccine safety, and were more likely to believe conspiracy theories about Covid-19 and Qanon. The same was true for people angry with Donald Trump; people angry at Trump were more likely to believe that he slowed the US mail for electoral advantage, that he suffered strokes while President, that he failed to send Covid investigators to China, and that Russia possessed a compromising video of Trump. For every claim, angry people were more misinformed.

Next, there was also a negative relationship between both use of conservative partisan media and belief accuracy, as well as use of liberal partisan media and belief accuracy. The data are clear: people who more frequently use conservative or liberal partisan media are more misinformed than those who use it less

Table 2 Between-person correlations for conservative partisan media use, anger, and belief accuracy.

	Evidence of voter fraud	Joe and Hunter Biden Ukraine scandal	Biden supports defunding police	Biden sexually assaulted former senate aide	Covid was planned	Facemask efficacy	Vaccine safety	Qanon
Between person correlation								
Conservative Partisan Media Use-Anger	.58***	.58***	.59***	.59***	.58***	.59***	.59***	.59***
Anger-Belief Accuracy	–.87***	–.73***	–.74***	–.77***	–.56***	–.67***	–.41***	–.68***
Conservative Partisan Media Use-Belief Accuracy	–.71***	–.63***	–.56***	–.51***	–.38***	–.51***	–.23***	–.50***

Note. *** p < .001.

Table 3 Between-person correlations for liberal partisan media use, anger, and belief accuracy.

	Trump slowed US mail	Trump suffered a series of strokes while in office	Trump sent researchers to China to investigate Covid	Trump Russia tape
Between person correlation				
Liberal Partisan Media Use-Anger	.67***	.68***	.67***	.68***
Anger-Belief Accuracy	−.89***	−.77***	−.77***	−.77***
Liberal Partisan Media Use-Belief Accuracy	−.66***	−.53***	−.54***	−.53***

frequently. These analyses highlight just how influential partisan media can be. Recall that I am looking at *everyone's* use of partisan media and not just Republicans using conservative media or Democrats using liberal media. I am not just examining selective exposure to like-minded sources but rather the influence of partisan media on anyone who encounters it. The fact that I find a direct relationship here – across all users – suggests that the problem is more about partisan media and less about echo chambers. Media content – not just biased processes of selection – matters here. It hints that any person who stumbles across partisan media could become more angry and misinformed by the content they see on these sites, *even if they are not politically aligned with the outlet*. Though audiences remain small, partisan media are influential because of the content they provide. The debate over echo chambers and like-minded media use may be distracting and diverting our attention from the very real problems of partisan media, namely it's content.

Taken together, these results paint a rather straightforward and concerning picture of the consequences of partisan media use. Users of partisan media – on both the left and the right – tend to be more politically angry and hold more misperceptions than their counterparts who do not typically use partisan media. More so, political anger can alter people's evaluations of the truth. Across all claims, people who were angrier at political opponents of the outlets were more likely to believe false, negative claims about those individuals (or reject the facts, in the case of Trump sending Covid investigators to China).

The data show that people who use partisan media feel differently and believe different things than less frequent or nonusers. But do partisan media change how people feel and what they believe? Do their levels of anger and misperceptions change over time as a result of using partisan media? This is an important question given what we know about how people select political media. Studies on selective exposure show that people have a preference for like-minded content (e.g. Garrett, 2009). These preferences raise questions about the causal nature of partisan media. If, for example, Republicans are more likely to use conservative partisan media outlets because those outlets reinforce their worldview, any observed effect of partisan media could be due to other factors that initially influenced media choice and not the content people are exposed to within partisan media. However, the RI-CLPM analyses used here are able to better isolate changes within individual people over time (Hamaker et al., 2015). In particular, the analyses allow for tests for fluctuations and deviations in individuals' baseline levels of anger and beliefs as a result of exposure to partisan media. In other words, it allows for more precise tests of whether people who use partisan media experiences changes in levels of anger and misperceptions over time. It also assesses whether changes in baseline anger and misperceptions drive people to use partisan media again in the future. Any significant relationship in the model can be interpreted as stronger causal evidence of change within individuals.

I illustrate the effects of partisan media use on anger and belief accuracy for each of the twelve claims in Figures 23–25. As I explain in further detail in the Appendix, given the short time period between waves, I work from the assumption that the effects from Wave 1 to Wave 2 are fairly similar to those between Waves 2 and 3. I therefore placed an equality constraint on the same paths across waves (see Orth et al., 2021). As a result, Figures 23–25 depict the relationships in two waves (t–1) and (t). In the figures themselves, solid lines indicate positive relationships, while dotted lines represent negative relationships.

I start by looking at the within-person effects of using conservative partisan media on anger at Joe Biden and belief in false claims about Biden and voter fraud in US elections. In all four models, the more people used conservative media the more angry they became at Biden over the course of the election. Further, the more angry individuals became at Biden the less accurate their beliefs were over the three waves of the study. Finally, did using conservative media directly make people more misinformed? For the three claims about Biden the answer is yes. Those who used more conservative media became less accurate in evaluating whether claims about Biden were true or not; but they did not seem to directly change users' beliefs about evidence of voter fraud over time, however. Overall, the findings indicate that using conservative media caused people to be more misinformed over the election, in part because it made audiences angry. This offers evidence of the power of conservative partisan media to arouse anger and mislead audiences.

The paths in Figure 23 suggest reciprocal or mutually reinforcing relationships as well. While partisan media increases anger and misperceptions, there is also evidence that people who are angry and misinformed also increased their use of conservative partisan media over the course of the election. This dynamic suggests an important and challenging feedback loop; people who use partisan news became more angry and misinformed, which further increases the likelihood that they use even more conservative news in the future. This process may in part be accounted for by identity threats; the more people use conservative partisan media the more their identities are heightened and the more angry and misinformed they become. As a result, they turn back to conservative partisan media to continue to monitor for identity threats (Young, 2023). In this way, use of conservative outlets leads to spiraling effects on anger and beliefs that serve to reinforce the use of partisan media (Slater, 2007).

The general finding that partisan media increase anger and misperceptions among audiences is also found for the claims about Covid, masking, and

Biden Sexually Assaulted Former Senate Aide

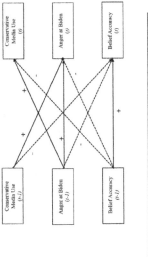

Joe and Hunter Biden Ukraine Scandal

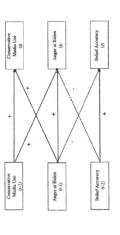

Biden Supports Defunding the Police

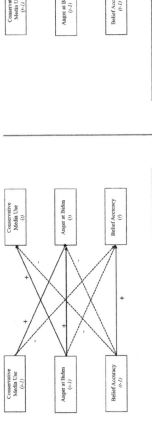

Evidence of Voter Fraud in U.S. Elections

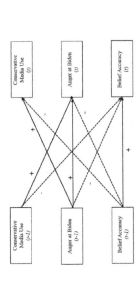

Figure 23 Path analyses for conservative media use, anger at Biden, and belief accuracy.

Note. Paths represent within person effects over time using RI-CLPMs. Paths are based on time invariant coefficients, as equality constraints were placed on the same path for the W1–W2 and W2–W3 relationships. Complete results from the RI-CLPMs from which the Figures are derived are found in Table A.6. Solid lines represent positive effects and dotted lines indicate negative effects.

Vaccines are generally safe and effective

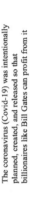

The coronavirus (Covid-19) was intentionally planned, created, and released so that billionaires like Bill Gates can profit from it

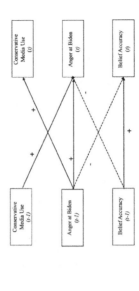

Facemasks are an effective measure in slowing the spread of COVID-19

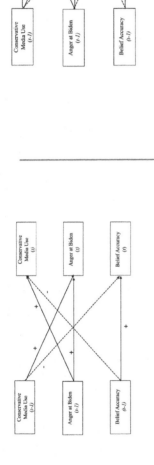

Donald Trump is fighting a group of politicians and celebrities who operate a child sex-trafficking ring

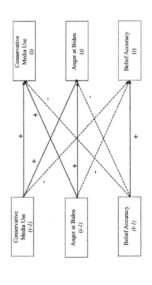

Figure 24 Path analyses for conservative media use, anger at Biden, and belief accuracy.

Note. Paths represent within person effects over time using RI-CLPMs. Paths are based on time invariant coefficients, as equality constraints were placed on the same path for the W1–W2 and W2–W3 relationships. Complete results from the RI-CLPMs from which the Figures are derived are found in Table A.7. Solid lines represent positive effects and dotted lines indicate negative effects.

Donald Trump ordered U.S. Postmaster General
Louis DeJoy to slow down mail services to help
Trump win the 2020 presidential election

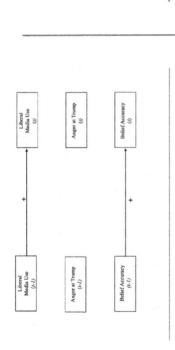

Donald Trump sought medical attention for a series of
strokes he has had while serving as president

The Trump administration attempted to get U.S. medical experts
into China to study the coronavirus outbreak in early 2020

The Russian government possesses a video tape of Donald
Trump with prostitutes in a Moscow hotel room in 2013

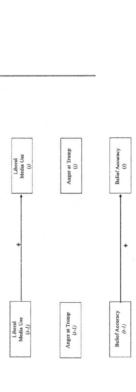

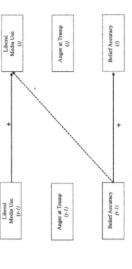

Figure 25 Path analyses for liberal media use, anger at Trump, and belief accuracy.

Note. Paths represent within person effects over time using RI-CLPMs. Paths are based on time invariant coefficients, as equality constraints were placed on
the same path for the W1–W2 and W2–W3 relationships. Complete results from the RI-CLPMs from which the Figures are derived are found in Table A.8.
Solid lines represent positive effects and dotted lines indicate negative effects.

vaccines. The paths in Figure 24 between use of conservative media and (a) anger and (b) belief accuracy indicate that users of conservative sites became angrier at Biden and more misinformed about these issue during the election. In most cases, angrier people also became more misinformed over time, suggesting that anger is a vital mechanism through which partisan media drive false beliefs. It is noteworthy that use of conservative partisan media did not directly change beliefs about Qanon during the election. It is unclear why this is the case. It could be that an extreme claim like the Qanon conspiracy was even outside the bounds of what many partisan media typically cover. Or it could be that audiences who are interested in or believe in Qanon used other online sources not measured in the survey.

The majority of the evidence from the Republican/conservative-aligned claims points to four important conclusions: (1) using conservative partisan media increases political anger, (2) using conservative partisan media promotes political misperceptions, (3) anger leads people to be more misinformed, and (4) both anger and false beliefs serve to further reinforce future use of conservative partisan media. This suggests that conservative partisan media have an important influence on how people feel about political figures and what they believe. These conservative sources are not innocuous but rather can stoke anger and alter beliefs.

What about liberal partisan media? I report above that audiences of liberal partisan media are more angry at Trump and more misinformed than people who don't use the sites frequently. But do users of liberal media become *more* angry and *more* misinformed over the election cycle as a result of using those sources? The answer, at least with the beliefs measured here, is no. For none of the four claims do we see a link (which represents change) between liberal partisan site use and anger or belief accuracy (see Figure 25). There is also no path between anger and beliefs. This should not be interpreted as evidence that liberal partisan media exert no influence on anger or misperceptions. They do, as people who use liberal media are more angry and more misinformed than people who don't. Rather, the missing paths in these analyses suggest that people who use liberal partisan media did not become angrier or more misinformed over the course of the 2020 election as a result of using liberal media. It is quite possible that those using liberal partisan media started the election very angry at and misinformed about Trump and further use of those sources did not boost already high levels of anger and misinformation. In this case, at least, using liberal media did not change how people felt about Trump or what they believed.

The differences in findings illustrate an important asymmetry in effects between using conservative and liberal partisan media. While users of partisan media are both more angry and misinformed, the evidence demonstrates that only use of conservative media changes people's emotions and beliefs during the election. This suggests that the content provided by online conservative media is creating anger and misperceptions in a way that liberal media outlets are not. This may be in part due to the highly emotional content on these sites (Berry & Sobieraj, 2013; Young, 2019), the cohesion in messages from conservative media online (Benkler et al., 2018), or the relatively high degree of misinformation circulating in more conservative corners of the internet (González-Bailón et al., 2023). Regardless of the cause, conservative media demonstrate more influence on audiences' anger and beliefs than do liberal sites.

6 Conclusion

Partisan media have become an important player in the American political media landscape. What started as syndicated conservative talk radio shows and a single, conservative cable television channel (*Fox News*) has morphed into a larger eco-system of both conservative and liberal partisan outlets online and on social media (Benkler et al., 2018; Hemmer, 2016; Peck, 2020). Partisan media are often the target of immense criticism and are frequently blamed by public commentators for a variety of America's political problems. This narrative often portrays audiences of partisan media as deeply entrenched in echo chambers, with little appetite for news or information that does not tell them exactly what they want to hear. Many critiques of partisan media have merit, but it is necessary to put partisan media and their audiences into proper context to understand their true scope and the influence in the American political system.

This Element examined a few central targets of criticism of partisan media: that their audiences are (1) very angry about politics; (2) politically misinformed and prone to believing conspiracy theories; and (3) that partisan media and anger drive those false beliefs. A comprehensive, multi-wave survey fielded during the 2020 US presidential election allowed me to examine who uses partisan media and how often, whether those audiences are angry, and how misinformed they are. It also allowed me to test whether using partisan media changes people's levels of anger and misperceptions during an election season, as well as differences in influence between conservative and liberal partisan media sites.

I found that people who used partisan media in the 2020 election were quite angry and believed a range of falsehoods, including claims about election fraud, politicians' policy positions, personal scandals, and health status, as well as misinformation about Covid, vaccines, and other conspiracy theories. In each and every case, the more people used partisan media, the more angry they were and the more they believed false claims about opposing politicians or issues. In some cases, these differences were stark, with the average user of partisan media being more *misinformed* than accurately informed.

That said, several important themes emerge here. The first is that audiences of partisan media remain relatively small, and most people *do not* use partisan media frequently, even in the context of a highly contentious and polarized presidential election. Despite widespread fears among scholars, pundits, and commentators, the evidence indicates that most people do not consume political information in partisan media echo chambers. People may occasionally seek or come across content from partisan media from time to time, but it is not a vital part of their media diet. More than 40% of people reported having never visited a liberal media outlet and nearly 50% reported having not seen content from a conservative media outlet. In fact, many people reported no news at all. These patterns are consistent with other research that uses behavioral measures to track partisan outlet use (Arguedas et al., 2022; Guess, 2021; Prior, 2013; Wojcieszak et al., 2023) and together a clear picture is starting to emerge: despite misguided assumptions about the size of partisan media audiences in the United States, the fact is that these audiences are small. Partisan media have not become deeply embedded in most Americans' lives or media habits.

However, that does not mean partisan media are inconsequential to American politics. Audiences for partisan media remain small, but it is also clear that those audiences think, feel, and behave differently than people who do not often use partisan media. We know that these audiences, particularly on the right, are highly engaged with partisan content, skilled at amplifying information online far beyond the original audiences. Content from partisan media, especially when it is emotional, is shared more widely than mainstream news and can spread rapidly through on online social networks. This is especially true for content from conservative media (Hasell, 2021; Hiaeshutter-Rice & Weeks, 2021; Wells et al., 2020; Zhang et al., 2023). The evidence from this Element suggests that we can also say that partisan media audiences are more angry and misinformed than others in society. Rather than dismissing the influence of partisan media because of relatively small audiences, we must instead pay attention to the ways in which those audiences are quite different from the larger public, particularly because of the potential influence these engaged individuals have over the larger political system (Prior, 2013).

People who use partisan media are angrier at political opponents – in this case the presidential candidate whose political affiliation is not in line with the ideology of the partisan media outlet. This is true for feelings about the leaders of both parties; users of conservative media were angrier at Joe Biden and users of liberal media were angrier with Donald Trump. While anger can at times be a healthy motivator of political behavior, it can also be problematic because it drives people to be even more partisan and, arguably, less rational. Angry people dig in on their prior beliefs and tend to see the world in a more partisan light (MacKuen et al., 2010; Weeks, 2015). And the evidence here makes clear that anger can lead people to believe things about politics, health, and science that are not true and were known to be false at the time. Anger played a significant role in shaping false beliefs about every one of the claims in the study. When people were angry at Biden or Trump, they believed things that were not true about them. In almost every instance, anger was a stronger predictor of misperceptions than was political party affiliation. This is not to say that partisanship is not a relevant factor in shaping people's (false) beliefs about politics. It most certainly is relevant. In particular, partisanship likely plays a vital role in triggering negative emotions like anger in the first place. So while partisanship is important for beliefs, clearly so too is anger.

Critically, anger also offers a compelling explanation for *why* partisan audiences are misinformed. Partisan media often use outrage as a market strategy to build an audience (e.g. Young, 2019). Audiences are subsequently exposed to some content that is intended to stoke anger. It works. But the outcomes of such exposure do not stop there. Those angry partisan audiences are subsequently more likely to accept political falsehoods as true. Anger is one important mechanism for why people become misinformed about politics; it reduces the likelihood that people engage in effortful and careful processing of information and instead makes them more reliant on partisan biases and motivations that leave them more susceptible to political falsehoods (MacKuen et al., 2010; Weeks, 2015).

Another theme that emerged from these data was the asymmetry in effects between conservative and liberal partisan media. Importantly, conservative partisan media exhibited a causal impact on audience members' anger and misperceptions in a way liberal media did not. Using conservative partisan media lead to changes in people's anger and beliefs. Over the course of the election, people who used conservative partisan media became angrier and more misinformed as a result of using these sources. The same pattern of causal change was not evident with liberal media. Why? The answer is two-fold.

First, there is growing evidence that liberal and conservative media ecosystems are not equivalent. The political right has established a more comprehensive and cohesive network of conservative media outlets that were born out of dissatisfaction with more mainstream sources (Benkler et al., 2018; Peck, 2020). These outlets promote themselves as alternative sources to what many users see as a liberal bias in news media and users look to these conservative media outlets to provide a counterweight to more mainstream sources (Pew,

2021). Some of these conservative sources have become among the most popular political information outlets in the US. Liberal partisan media do not have a similar network of trusted partisan outlets.

This may in part help explain why the relationships between conservative partisan media use, anger, and misperceptions, represent a reinforcing spiral or feedback loop (Slater, 2007). As noted, I found that conservative site users became angrier and more misinformed over the course of the election. At the same time, anger and false beliefs only make people *more likely* to use conservative partisan media again in the future. In a way, angry and misinformed people seek out conservative sources that reinforce their anger and help justify their beliefs. Although I am not able to untangle why angry and misinformed audiences return to conservative partisan media, we know some audiences are drawn to conservative content that stokes anger, perhaps as a form of identity expression or group attachment (Berry & Sobieraj, 2013; Webster, 2020; Young, 2019). The political right in the United States is more homogeneous than the left and it may be that conservative sources speak to and connect with their audiences' identities in a way that liberal outlets do not (Pew, 2023; Young, 2023). It may also be that angry and misinformed people return to conservative partisan sources because they trust them more than mainstream sources. There is some evidence that conservative audiences find these sources to be more credible and trustworthy than nonpartisan sources, which can help explain why they use them (Hmielowski et al., 2022; Metzger et al., 2020; Pew, 2021; Tsfati & Cappella, 2003). If that's the case, breaking the reinforcing cycle of conservative media and influence would be very difficult. If committed users trust conservative partisan media, and the content reinforces existing beliefs and helps justify political anger and false beliefs, conservative media may have a stronghold on its small but loyal audiences. Why would someone go elsewhere for political information?

Second, the nature of content in liberal and conservative media outlets may be qualitatively different. Conservative partisan media often present themselves as a voice of the people, taking a populist tone to covering news and politics (Peck, 2020). Conservative media often use outrage and anger as a tactic to attract audiences, whereas liberal media often take a satirical approach that attempts to critique through irony and humor (Berry & Sobieraj, 2013; Webster, 2020; Young, 2019). The approach of conservative media appears to work, as audiences are drawn to and engage with more extreme conservative content (Benkler et al., 2018; Garrett & Bond, 2021; Hasell, 2021; Hiaeshutter-Rice & Weeks, 2021; Wells et al., 2020; Zhang et al., 2023). There is also evidence that conservative media devotes significant coverage to misinformation (Benkler et al., 2018; Broockman & Kalla, 2023; González-Bailón et al., 2023; Jamieson et al.,

2023). It may be that audiences of conservative outlets are exposed to more misinformation than are audiences of liberal media. This is an important question that needs more examination moving forward, as there are relatively few systematic analyses of differences in content between liberal and conservative media.

While I do find that conservative partisan media have asymmetrical (i.e. stronger) effects on audiences than liberal partisan media, this does not mean that liberal outlets do not anger or misinform consumers. The liberal partisan media ecosphere is not as powerful or influential as the conservative one in spreading information and setting media agendas (Benkler et al., 2018; Vargo et al., 2018), but audiences of liberal media were angrier at Trump and more likely to believe falsehoods about him relative to non- or less-frequent users of liberal media. The fact that levels of anger or misperceptions among audiences for liberal media did not change over the election does not mean that liberal media have no influence. Rather, it could mean that users of liberal media started the election angry at and misinformed about Trump and didn't change in one direction or another. Given that Trump was the incumbent and in office for nearly four years, many users of liberal partisan media may have already been extremely angry at Trump for years. In this way, liberal media could have contributed to stability in anger and false beliefs, simply reinforcing those feelings and views. But the lack of change observed among those who used liberal media could also indicate something fundamentally different about either the nature of liberal partisan content relative to conservative content or their audiences. As noted, it is possible that the way in which conservative media cover stories surrounding false claims is qualitatively different than the way liberal media cover them. It is also possible that conservative audiences put more weight in what they see in conservative outlets, particularly given their high levels of trust in outlets like *Fox News* (Pew, 2020). In other words, there is the potential that audiences of conservative media are more likely than liberal audiences to incorporate the information they see in conservative media when forming beliefs. Neither of these alternative possibilities can be tested with the data here but illustrate important questions that need to be addressed in future research.

What does all of this mean for how we think about the role partisan media play in American politics? First, it indicates that audiences of partisan news are different from the general public. They are no doubt small relative to the larger US population. But partisan media introduce a difficult challenge to democracy and society: these audiences are relatively small but they are highly engaged, interested, angry, and often wrong. They amplify content online at a greater rate than audiences for nonpartisan news. What this means is that partisan content, which at times is biased, misleading, or outright wrong, has the opportunity to spread far beyond its original audience, thus potentially having indirect reach and influence (Druckman et al., 2018).

It is important to note that this study took place in the context of the 2020 US presidential election, which was one of the most contentious and divisive elections in recent American history. It also took place during a global pandemic, at a time of economic uncertainty, and in the aftermath of significant protests for racial and social justice. Anger at both candidates (and the political system) was high throughout the election, misinformation circulated in many online spaces, not just in partisan media, and people were likely consuming more media than they usually do. One could argue that the unique context of the election contributed to the findings. This is a possibility but the reality in contemporary American politics is that voters are polarized and hold strong, negative feelings toward political opponents (Iyengar et al., 2019). Anecdotally, little has changed politically since the fall of 2020 in the United States; the public is still angry at political opponents, political misinformation still circulates, and partisan media are still relevant. And given the likelihood of a rematch between Trump and Biden in the 2024 election, the results here are not likely to have been entirely driven by the timing of the study. This type of environment may be the new normal for American politics.

This Element began by noting that people in the United States are angry and in some cases misinformed about politics. The causes of this anger and these misperceptions are diverse and include cultural, political, and technological changes in our society. The analyses here provide a more lucid picture of one source of influence: online partisan media. Audiences of partisan media, though small, are important. They are angrier and, ultimately, more misinformed. While it is vitally important not to exaggerate the power of partisan media in shaping citizens' emotions and beliefs – particularly in the context of small audiences – it is also necessary to recognize that partisan media are not harmless. They matter. The content they produce matters. They can motivate audiences to take action based on falsehoods or conspiracy theories, as we saw with the destruction at the US Capitol on January 6, 2021. But studying partisan audiences is also a moving target and pinpointing its influence may become harder in the future as more partisan outlets and sources emerge online and on social media. The growing partisan media ecosystem includes podcasters, influencers, activists, and other opinion leaders who operate outside traditional journalistic institutions and without editorial standards. In this crowded information environment, traditional and alternative news media compete for limited audiences all while technology (and algorithms) may become increasingly important in the types of information we see online. Partisan media have already become adept at using these systems to their advantage. Understanding the role partisan media play now and in the future remains a fundamental question for political communication.

Appendix of Methodological Details

A.1 Data and Sample Characteristics

To test the reciprocal relationships between partisan media exposure, political anger, and political misperceptions, I use data from an original, three wave panel survey I fielded in the United States during the 2020 election. I contracted the research company YouGov to field the survey on my behalf and the sample was drawn from YouGov's web access panel. YouGov uses a stratified sampling approach with matching on gender, race, age, and education (based on the 2018 American Community Survey) to obtain samples from non-randomly selected pools of respondents. Although the sample is not strictly representative, the matching methodology creates samples that closely reflect the target population on key demographics and are a reasonable approximation of samples drawn using true probabilistic approaches.

The first wave of the study was fielded between September 24 and October 5, 2020. YouGov invited 5,298 individuals to take part in the study and 2070 finished the first wave of the survey for a completion rate of 39.1%. Of the 2070 people who completed Wave 1, 270 were removed by YouGov to meet quota sampling requirements and ensure the sample reflects the population of American adults. The final sample size in Wave 1 was 1,800. The second wave of the survey was fielded several weeks after the first and data were collected between October 22 and 30. A total of 1401 respondents completed Wave 2 for a retention rate of 77.83%. The final wave of data was collected between November 19 and 24, 2020, a few weeks after the election. A total of 1,065 respondents completed wave three (59.2% of respondents finished all three waves). One respondent reported using every media outlet in all waves and was omitted from the main analyses later.

The sample reflected the American population on several key demographics. The mean age of respondents was 50.28 (16.97) years and 55.7% were women. In terms of race, 76.1% of respondents were White, 8.2% Black, 7.6% Hispanic, 2.2% Asian, 0.8% Native American, and additional 5.2% identified as biracial or another unlisted race. The mean education level was 3.5 (SD = 1.48) on a 6-point scale, which falls between "some college" and "2-year degree." The mean income level was 6.44 (SD = 3.56) on a 16-point scale, which translates to the average sample income falling between $50,000 and $69,999. Finally, 35.8% of respondents identified as Democrats, 30.3% as politically Independent, and 24.9% as Republicans.

A.2 Description of Variables

A.2.1 Partisan Media Use

Asking people to self-report media use is a historically difficult task, as they tend to overestimate the frequency with which they use media or visit different sources (Scharkow, 2019). To better minimize response bias, I applied a version of the 'list-frequency' technique to measure exposure to these outlets. As the name suggests, the list-frequency approach provides a list of very specific outlets and asks respondents to identify the sources used in a set period of time, as well as the frequency of that use. The idea is that respondents are able to identify specific sources recently used and can provide reasonably accurate estimates of the frequency of that use. This approach is recommended for self-report measures of media use (Andersen et al., 2016).

In each wave of the survey, respondents were presented with the list of sources and asked to select any sources they had used at least once in the past fourteen days for news or political information. The order of presentation was randomized across all sources and the lists were broken up into several pages to prevent response fatigue. Respondents only selected the sources they had used and did not need to respond or check 'no' for unused sources. After completing the entire battery of source questions, respondent who noted that they had used a specific source were brought to a second page that asked them how often they used the sources they indicated they had used. If, for example, a respondent said they only used *Fox News* in the prior two weeks, they were only asked about their frequency of *Fox News* use. Respondents who used more than one source were asked about frequency of use for each individual source. Respondents were asked on a 7-point scale "how often have you used the sources listed below to get news or information about politics in the past 14 days?" Reponses options included (1) Never, (2) Once, (3) Once per week, (4) A few times per week, (5) Several times per week, (6) Every day, and (7) Several times a day. If a respondent did not report using a particular source, their frequency score for that sources was coded as (1) 'Never.' Frequency of use for each type of news (nonpartisan, liberal partisan, conservative partisan) was calculated by taking the average frequency of use for each site within the category.

The site categorization process is described in the main text. As noted, *CNN* was coded as a liberal site. The decision where to place *CNN* has been found to have implications for studies examining partisan media diets. For example, Muise et al. (2022) find that partisan segregation in television news audiences is considerably more pronounced for left-leaning media if *CNN* is counted as a partisan rather than a mainstream source. If *CNN* is categorized as liberal partisan media, they find that partisan segregation on the left more closely resembles segregation on the right. Given the possibility that the categorization of *CNN* could dramatically change the interpretation of the analyses in this Element, I reran all of the RI-CLPM models with a measure of liberal partisan media that excluded *CNN*. All other aspects of the analyses were the same. The findings from the models with *CNN* not included as a liberal partisan outlet are nearly identical to those with *CNN* included. The only notable difference is that the link between partisan media exposure and belief accuracy for the claim that Trump slowed down the mail for electoral advantage becomes significant in the model without *CNN*. For the rest of the models, the findings are similar and none of the interpretations about the influence of liberal partisan media on political anger or misperceptions change; with or without *CNN* included as a partisan media outlet, I find that liberal partisan users are angrier and more misinformed than less frequent users, but that liberal media did not change levels of political anger or misperceptions over the election.

A.2.2 Political Anger

The anger measure was designed to assess respondents' levels of anger directed at the two major party candidates for president, Donald Trump and Joe Biden. In each wave, respondents were asked to report the extent to which they felt a range of emotions toward Trump and Biden. They were provided a prompt that read "When I think about Donald Trump/Joe Biden, I feel . . . " followed by several emotions, including angry and mad. Responses were measured on a 7-point scale (1=not at all, 2=slightly, 3=somewhat, 4=moderately, 5=quite a bit, 6=very, 7=extremely). In each wave the angry and mad items were combined to create unique anger scales for both Trump and Biden.

A.2.3 Political Misperceptions

In most cases, beliefs were measured on a 5-point scale (1= Definitely true, 2 = Probably true, 3 = Probably false, 4 = Definitely false, 5 = Unsure). Based on the particular claim in question, responses were recoded such that higher values reflect more accurate answers. Unsure responses were coded as the midpoint (3). For the items about Covid, vaccines, and election fraud, the question approach was slightly different. For these questions, respondents were provided two opposite statements and asked to place a mark on a 5-point scale that best described their personal beliefs. For example, the voter fraud question provided two statements "There is no evidence of widespread voter fraud in U.S. elections" and "There is evidence of widespread voter fraud in U.S. elections" and placed a mark closer to which one they believed. Responses were recoded such that higher scores reflect more accurate beliefs about the statements.

A.3 Analysis Plan

One common way to model media effects over time with longitudinal panel survey data is using a cross-lagged panel model (CLPM). CLPMs use cross-lagged auto-regressive analyses to assess reciprocal relationships between variables in a model and provide evidence of the causal influence variables have on each other over time. In simple terms, CLPMs examine the effect of variable X on variable Y, while controlling for prior measures of variable Y. If the data show that variable X in Time 1 has an effect on variable Y in Time 2, after accounting for values of variable Y in Time 1, then the relationship between X and Y can be considered causal. However, CLPMs have recently been criticized for a few key limitations. The major concern with CLPMs is that they do not distinguish between-person differences from changes within individuals over time (Hamaker et al, 2015). However, the distinction is often critically important to media effects research. A within-person effect is a pattern of change within individuals and suggests a causal relationship between media exposure and effect, while between-person effects illustrate whether patterns of media use are associated with key outcomes over time (Thomas et al., 2021). Because CLPMs do not disaggregate the two types of effects, these models can lead to misleading conclusions about the effects of media.

To address the shortcomings of the CLPM, researchers have recently turned to random-intercept cross-lagged panel models (RI-CLPM). RI-CLPM overcome the limitations of CLPM by separating within- and between-person effects. Such an approach is particularly well-suited to test media effects models within the reinforcing spiral framework (Slater et al., 2020). The cross-lagged paths in the model represent the test of the study's hypotheses.

The RI-CLPMs use all three waves of data and are designed to better assess causality by separating out the between and within-subject effects using a random intercept (Hamaker et al., 2015). The between-subject effects represent stable between-person differences. The within-person effects assess change in an individual over time, while controlling for trait-like differences at the between person level. These within-person effects allow for the assessment of reciprocal relationships across waves.

To be clear, the between-subject effects in the RI-CLPMs test (1) whether people who use more partisan media are angrier than people who use less, (2) whether people who use more partisan media are more misinformed than people who use less, and (3) whether people who are angrier are more misinformed. The reported correlations for the between-person components represent stable, between-person differences. The within-subjects effects test whether an increase from an individual's baseline level of variable A leads to a change from baseline for that individual on variable B at time 2. For example, I test whether an increase from an individual's baseline use of partisan media in Wave 1 causes a change from baseline in anger and misperceptions in W2 (and so on). Again, these within-individual models automatically control for all unmeasured, time-invariant variables that could confound the relationship.

The modeling approach to the RI-CLPM I used here closely follows recent recommendations (see Hamaker et al., 2015; Mulder & Hamaker, 2021) and replicates the modeling strategy from other studies in communication science that employ the RI-CLPM (e.g. Baumgartner et al., 2018; Schnauber-Stockmann et al., 2021). I regressed the repeated measures for partisan media use, political anger, and belief accuracy on latent variables for each and fixed all factor loadings to 1. To assess both the within- and between-individual variance, the variances of the manifest variables were constrained to zero (see Baumgartner et al., 2018; Mulder & Hamaker, 2021). I also added a random intercept for each and constrained the factors loadings to 1. The complete empirical model for the RI-CLPMs is depicted in Figure A.1.

The resulting models test both within- and between-person effects. The coefficients for the auto-regressive paths (e.g. Wave 1 anger to Wave 2 anger) represent carry-over effects within people. For example, a positive coefficient across waves for political anger indicates that people experiencing more anger relative to their own expected score on anger are likely to experience elevated anger at a subsequent wave as well. The cross-lagged coefficients indicate the effects of one variable on another over time. A negative cross-lagged coefficient between anger and belief accuracy provides evidence of an effect of anger on belief accuracy; a deviation in an individuals' baseline level of anger leads to less belief accuracy compared to that individual's expected baseline level of accuracy (Mulder & Hamaker, 2021). The between-person effects are evident in the correlation between the random intercepts.

In all of the models, the auto-regressive and cross-lagged panel models were constrained to be equal across waves. This approach is recommended when lags between waves of data collection are approximately the same length. Implementing equality constraints across waves is advantageous in such instances because it increases the power of significance tests, improves model convergence, and reduces the complexity of results (see Orth et al., 2021). The latter benefit eliminates the challenge of offering explanations for between-interval differences in effects. In all cases I compared the model fit of the constrained model to the unconstrained model. In only one instance (US voter fraud) did the unconstrained model fit significantly better than the constrained model. Note that the cross-wave equity constraints are imposed on the unstandardized coefficients. The standardized coefficients reported in the book from the RI-CLPM are an average of the coefficients from W1 to W2 and W2 to W3.

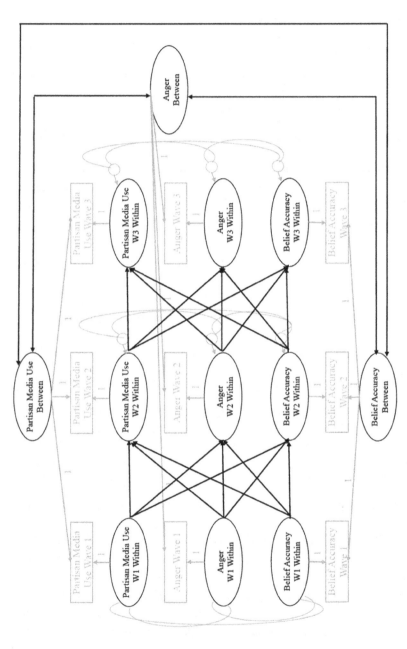

Figure A.1 Random Intercept Cross-Lagged Panel Model (RI-CLPM) representing relationship between partisan media use, political anger, and belief accuracy across three waves.

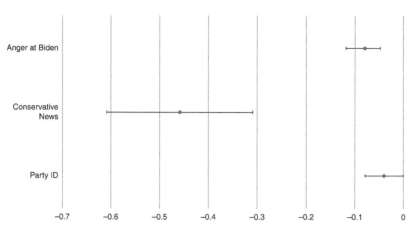

Figure A.2a Anger, Conservative Media, and Party ID as Predictors of Misperceptions (Biden Ukraine Scandal).

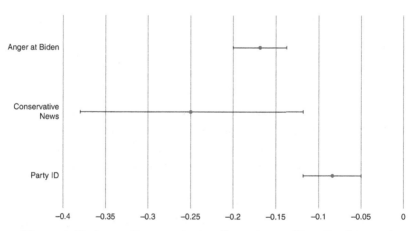

Figure A.2b Anger, Conservative Media, and Party ID as Predictors of Misperceptions (Biden Sexual Assault).

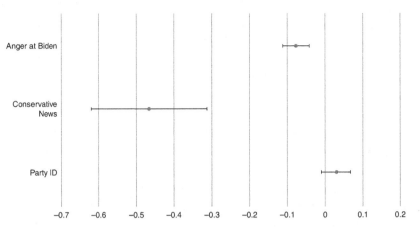

Figure A.2c Anger, Conservative Media, and Party ID as Predictors of Misperceptions (Qanon).

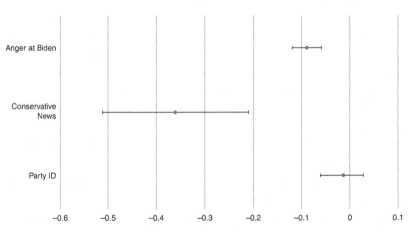

Figure A.3a Anger, Conservative Media, and Party ID as Predictors of Misperceptions (Covid Was Planned).

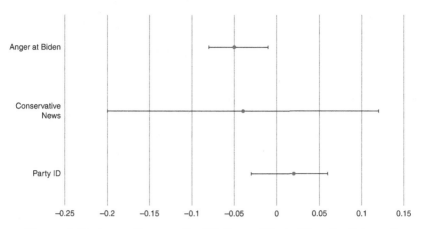

Figure A.3b Anger, Conservative Media, and Party ID as Predictors of
Misperceptions (Vaccines are Safe).

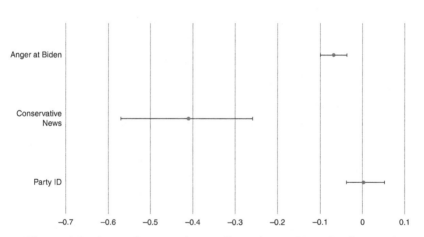

Figure A.3c Anger, Conservative Media, and Party ID as Predictors of
Misperceptions (Facemask Efficacy).

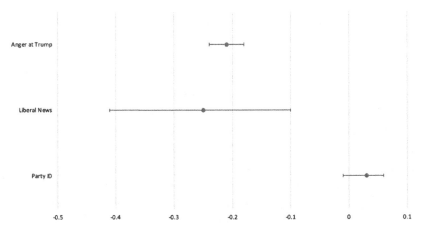

Figure A.4a Anger, Liberal Media, and Party ID as Predictors of Misperceptions (Trump Russia Tape).

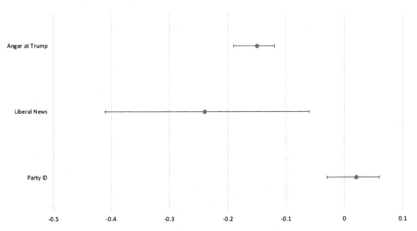

Figure A.4b Anger, Liberal Media, and Party ID as Predictors of Misperceptions (Trump Sent COVID Investigators to China).

Table A.1 Predicting News Site Use in Wave 1

	Nonpartisan news use	Conservative news use	Liberal news use
Conservative news site use	.22(.04)***	–	.11(.02)***
Liberal news site use	.97(.03)***	.14(.03)***	–
Nonpartisan news site use	–	.12(.02)***	.38(.01)***
Anger toward Joe Biden	−.01(.01)#	.02(.01)**	−.01(.01)
Anger toward Donald Trump	.02(.01)*	−.04(.01)***	.01(.01)
Party ID (rep. coded high)	.01(.01)	.01(.01)	−.01(.01)#
Ideology (conservative coded high)	−.01(.02)	.07(.01)***	−.04(.01)***
Political interest	.03(.02)#	.04(.01)***	.02(.01)*
Political knowledge	.02(.01)	.00(.01)	−.01(.01)
Distrust of mainstream media	−.07(.01)***	.05(.01)***	−.01(.01)
Social media for political information	.00(.01)	.02(.01)***	.01(.00)
Political expression on social media	.03(.01)*	.03(.01)***	.01(.01)*
Age	.00(.00)	.00(.00)	.00(.00)
Gender (women coded high)	−.07(.03)**	−.02(.02)	.02(.02)
Education	.04(.01)***	.01(.01)	−.02(.01)**
Asian	.11(.08)	.05(.06)	−.06(.05)
Black	−.05(.05)	.07(.04)#	.05(.03)
Hispanic	−.01(.05)	.08(.03)*	−.01(.03)
Multi-racial/other races	.09(.05)	.05(.04)	−.01(.03)
Constant	.06(.11)	.21(.08)**	.49(.07)***
R^2 *(F)*	.63(137.96)***	.43(61.09)***	.61(125.95)***
(df)	1495	1495	1495

Note. Unstandardized coefficients reported. Standard errors in parentheses.
***$p \leq .001$, **$p \leq .01$, *$p \leq .05$, #$p \leq .10$ (all p values two-tailed).

Table A.2 Predicting Political Anger in Wave 1

	Anger toward Joe Biden	Anger toward Donald Trump
Conservative news site use	.33(.12)**	−.78(.11)***
Liberal news site use	−.14(.14)	.15(.13)
Nonpartisan news site use	−.15(.09)#	.19(.08)*
Anger toward Joe Biden	−	−.07(.03)**
Anger toward Donald Trump	−.08(.03)**	−
Party ID (rep. coded high)	.29(.03)***	−.47(.03)***
Ideology (conservative coded high)	−.07(.05)	−.38(.05)***
Political interest	.28(.05)***	.09(.05)#
Political knowledge	−.10(.04)*	.14(.04)***
Distrust of mainstream media	.37(.03)***	−.25(.03)***
Social media for political information	−.03(.02)	.02(.02)
Political expression on social media	.15(.03)***	.10(.03)***
Age	.00(.00)	.00(.00)
Gender (women coded high)	−.08(.08)	.22(.08)**
Education	−.02(.03)	.07(.03)*
Asian	.02(.27)	−.17(.25)
Black	−.20(.16)	−.24(.15)
Hispanic	.06(.15)	.05(.15)
Multi-racial/other races	.34(.18)#	−.03(.17)
Constant	−.41(.35)	7.29(.27)***
R^2 *(F)*	.51(84.87)***	.70(191.03)***
(df)	1495	1495

Note. Unstandardized coefficients reported. Standard errors in parentheses.
***$p \leq .001$, **$p \leq .01$, *$p \leq .05$, #$p \leq .10$ (all p values two-tailed).

Table A.3 Predicting Political Misperceptions

	Biden sexually assaulted former senate aide	Joe and Hunter Biden Ukraine scandal	Biden supports defunding police	Evidence of voter fraud in US elections
Conservative news site use	−.25(.07)***	−.46(.08)***	−.49(.078)***	−.51(.08)***
Liberal news site use	.29(.07)***	.34(.09)***	.30(.09)***	.26(.09)**
Nonpartisan news site use	.04(.05)	.10(.05)#	.12(.06)*	.14(.06)*
Anger toward Joe Biden	−.17(.01)***	−.08(.02)***	−.10(.02)***	−.09(.02)***
Anger toward Donald Trump	.11(.02)***	.13(.02)***	.17(.02)***	.10(.02)***
Party ID (rep. coded high)	−.09(.02)***	−.04(.02)#	−.06(.02)**	−.02(.02)
Ideology (conservative coded high)	.17(.03)***	.00(.03)	−.02(.03)	−.12(−.04)***
Political interest	.04(.03)	−.01(.03)	.01(.03)	−.02(.04)
Political knowledge	−.01(.02)	−.01(.03)	.15(.03)***	.20(.03)***
Distrust of mainstream media	−.16(.02)***	−.17(.02)***	−.15(.02)***	−.23(.02)***

Table A.3 (cont.)

	Biden sexually assaulted former senate aide	Joe and Hunter Biden Ukraine scandal	Biden supports defunding police	Evidence of voter fraud in US elections
Social media for political information	-.02(.01)	.01(.01)	.01(.02)	-.01(.02)
Political expression on social media	-.01(.02)	-.02(.02)	-.04(.02)#	-.03(.02)
Age	.01(.00)***	.00(.00)	.00(.00)	.00(.00)
Gender (women coded high)	-.01(.05)	-.05(.05)	-.23(.06)***	-.08(.06)
Education	-.03(.02)#	.02(.02)	.02(.02)	.00(.02)
Asian	-.22(.15)	.09(.15)	-.09(.17)	-.29(.18)
Black	.02(.09)	.09(.10)	.06(.10)	-.17(.11)
Hispanic	-.02(.08)	.10(.10)	-.08(.10)	-.35(.10)***
Multi-racial/other races	-.05(.10)	-.23(.11)*	-.07(.12)	-.29(.12)*
Constant	3.07(.19)***	3.27(.22)***	3.20(.23)***	4.39(.23)***
R^2 (F)	.58(106.84)***	.54(92.31)***	.60(117.58)***	.59(111.89)***
(df)	1495	1495	1495	1495

Note. Unstandardized coefficients reported. Standard errors in parentheses. Higher values reflect more accurate beliefs. ***$p \leq$ .001, **$p \leq$ .01, *$p \leq$ .05, #$p \leq$ .10 (all p values two-tailed).

Table A.4 Predicting Political Misperceptions

	Vaccine safety	Mask efficacy	Covid was planned	Qanon
Conservative news site use	−.04(.08)	−.41(.08)***	−.36(.08)***	−.46(.08)***
Liberal news site use	−.05(.09)	.05(.09)	.00(.09)	.10(.09)
Nonpartisan news site use	.08(.06)	.16(.06)**	.11(.06)#	.18(.06)***
Anger toward Joe Biden	−.05(.02)**	−.07(.02)***	−.09(.02)***	−.07(.02)***
Anger toward Donald Trump	.05(.02)**	.12(.02)***	.03(.02)#	.11(.02)***
Party ID (rep. coded high)	.02(.02)	.00(.02)	−.01(.02)	.03(.02)
Ideology (conservative coded high)	−.12(.04)***	−.12(.04)***	−.07(.03)#	−.15(.04)***
Political interest	.08(.04)*	.04(.04)	.04(.03)	.04(.04)
Political knowledge	.11(.03)***	.02(.03)	.23(.03)***	.20(.03)***
Distrust of mainstream media	−.09(.02)***	−.16(.02)***	−.12(.02)***	−.13(.02)***
Social media for political information	−.04(.02)*	−.02(.02)	−.03(.01)*	−.03(.02)#
Political expression on social media	−.06(.02)*	−.07(.02)***	−.07(.02)***	−.05(.02)*
Age	.00(.00)	.00(.00)	.00(.00)	.00(.00)
Gender (women coded high)	−.11(.06)#	.00(.06)	−.16(.05)**	−.14(.06)*
Education	.10(.02)***	.02(.02)	.09(.02)***	.05(.02)**
Asian	−.08(.18)	.39(.18)*	−.20(.17)	.02(.18)
Black	−.75(.11)***	.10(.11)	−.41(.10)***	−.02(.11)
Hispanic	−.14(.11)	.08(.10)	−.02(.10)	.00(.10)
Multi-racial/other races	−.20(.12)	−.09(.12)	−.17(.11)	−.06(.12)
Constant	4.01(.24)***	4.75(.23)***	4.42(.22)	3.81(.23)***
R^2 (F)	.27(28.80)***	.49(73.33)***	.40(52.52)***	.50(77.10)***
(df)	1494	1493	1495	1495

Note. Unstandardized coefficients reported. Standard errors in parentheses. Higher values reflect more accurate beliefs. ***$p \leq .001$, **$p \leq .01$, *$p \leq .05$, #$p \leq .10$ (all p values two-tailed).

Table A.5 Predicting Political Misperceptions

	Trump deliberately slowed US mail	Trump suffered strokes while President	Trump attempts to get US researchers into China	Trump Russia tape
Conservative news site use	.26(.06)***	.28(.07)***	.45(.08)***	.25(.07)***
Liberal news site use	−.38(.07)***	−.37(.08)***	−.24(.09)**	−.25(.08)***
Nonpartisan news site use	.11(.05)*	−.01(.05)	.01(.06)	.01(.05)
Anger toward Joe Biden	.09(.01)***	.06(.02)***	.05(.02)**	.08(.02)***
Anger toward Donald Trump	−.27(.02)***	−.14(.02)***	−.15(.02)***	−.21(.02)***
Party ID (rep. coded high)	.06(.02)***	.05(.02)**	.02(.02)	.03(.02)
Ideology (conservative coded high)	.08(.03)**	−.02(.03)	.00(.04)	.03(.03)
Political interest	.00(.03)	.04(.03)	.09(.04)*	.10(.03)***
Political knowledge	.07(.02)***	.12(.03)***	−.04(.03)	.15(.02)***
Distrust of mainstream media	.0(.02)***	.03(.02)#	.07(.02)***	.04(.02)*
Social media for political information	.01(.01)	−.03(.01)*	−.01(.02)	.02(.01)
Political expression on social media	−.04(.02)*	.00(.02)	−.03(.02)	−.03(.02)
Age	−.00(.00)*	.00(.00)	.00(.00)	.00(.00)
Gender (women coded high)	.03(.05)	−.07(.05)	.01(.06)	−.12(.05)*
Education	.03(.02)*	−.01(.02)	.04(.02)#	.02(.02)

Asian	−.40(.14)**	−.04(.16)	−.11(.18)	−.01(.15)
Black	−.40(.09)***	−.12(.09)	.06(.11)	−.27(.09)**
Hispanic	−.04(.08)	−.06(.09)	−.25(.10)*	.00(.09)
Multi-racial/other races	−.09(.09)	−.02(.10)	−.13(.12)	.09(.10)
Constant	2.91(.19)***	3.34(.20)***	2.65(.23)***	2.74(.20)***
R^2 (F)	.71(187.96)***	.41(54.68)***	.37(44.92)***	.54(90.05)***
(df)	1495	1495	1495	1495

Note. Unstandardized coefficients reported. Standard errors in parentheses. Higher values reflect more accurate beliefs. ***$p \leq .001$, **$p \leq .01$, *$p \leq .05$, #$p \leq .10$ (all p values two-tailed).

Table A.6 Predicting Conservative Partisan Media Use, Anger at Biden, and Belief Accuracy

	Evidence of voter fraud in 2020 election		Joe and Hunter Biden Ukraine scandal		Biden supports defunding police		Biden sexually assaulted former senate aide	
	b (s.e.)	β	b (s.e.)	β	b (s.e.)	β	b (s.e.)	β
Effects on Conservative Media Use								
Conservative Media Use (Autoregressive)	.11 (.05)*	.12	.09 (.05)#	.09	.05 (.06)	.06	.09 (.05)#	.09
Anger at Biden (Cross-Lagged)	.21 (.04)***	.21	.14 (.04)***	.14	.11 (.05)*	.11	.15 (.05)***	.15
Belief Accuracy (Cross-Lagged)	−.06 (.05)	−.05	−.28 (.05)***	−.20	−.32 (.06)***	−.22	−.31 (.07)***	−.19
Effects on Anger at Biden								
Anger at Biden (Autoregressive)	.32 (.04)***	.29	.22 (.05)***	.20	.21 (.06)***	.19	.26 (.05)***	.24
Conservative Media Use (Cross-Lagged)	.17 (.04)***	.16	.12 (.04)***	.12	.10 (.04)*	.09	.14 (.04)***	.13
Belief Accuracy (Cross-Lagged)	−.11 (.04)**	−.09	−.27 (.05)***	−.19	−.25 (.06)***	−.17	−.16 (.07)***	−.09
Effects on Belief Accuracy								
Belief Accuracy (Autoregressive)	.33 (.04)***	.32	.18 (.04)***	.17	.17 (.06)**	.16	.18 (.05)***	.17
Conservative Media Use (Cross-Lagged)	−.05 (.03)#	−.06	−.15 (.05)***	−.20	−.12 (.03)***	−.18	−.10 (.02)***	−.15
Anger at Biden (Cross-Lagged)	−.17 (.03)***	−.18	−.20 (.03)***	−.25	−.09 (.03)**	−.12	−.10 (.03)***	−.16

Between Person Correlation

Conservative Media Use–Anger	.58***	.58***	.59***	.59***
Anger-Belief Accuracy	-.87***	-.73***	-.74***	-.77***
Conservative Media Use-Belief Accuracy	-.71***	-.63***	-.56***	-.51***
Fit Indices				
RMSEA	.10	.00	.01	.00
CFI	.98	1.0	1.0	1.0
TLI	.95	1.0	1.0	1.0
χ^2 (df)	146.44 (12)	12.27 (12)	14.16 (12)	11.44 (12)

Note. *** $p < .001$, ** $p < .01$, * $p < .05$, # $p < .001$. Reported standardized coefficients are the averaged path for W1-W2 and W2-W3 (see Orth et al., 2021 for details). Results from RI-CLPMs for each outcome variable. For belief accuracy, more accurate beliefs are coded higher.

Table A.7 Predicting Conservative Media Use, Anger at Biden, and Belief Accuracy

	Covid was planned		Face mask efficacy		Qanon		Vaccine safety	
	b (s.e.)	β	*b (s.e.)*	β	*b (s.e.)*	β	*b (s.e.)*	β
Effects on Conservative Media Use								
Conservative Media Use (Autoregressive)	.12(.05)*	.12	.12(.05)*	.12	.09(.06)#	.10	.11(.06)#	.11
Anger at Biden (Cross-Lagged)	.20(.04)***	.20	.18(.04)***	.17	.17(.04)***	.18	.20(.05)	.20
Belief Accuracy (Cross-Lagged)	-.12(.07)#	-.07	-.26(.07)***	-.17	-.10(.07)	-.08	-.20(.08)**	-.12
Effects on Anger at Biden								
Anger at Biden (Autoregressive)	.28(.05)***	.26	.22(.05)***	.20	.29(.05)***	.27	.31(.05)***	.28
Conservative Media Use (Cross-Lagged)	.17(.04)***	.16	.14(.04)***	.14	.15(.04)***	.14	.16(.04)***	.15
Belief Accuracy (Cross-Lagged)	-.27(.07)***	-.14	-.31(.06)***	-.20	-.21(.06)***	-.14	-.06(.07)	-.03
Effects on Belief Accuracy								
Belief Accuracy (Autoregressive)	.13(.06)*	.12	.23(.06)***	.22	.21(.06)***	.21	.15(.07)*	.15
Conservative Media Use (Cross-Lagged)	-.08(.03)***	-.13	-.10(.03)***	-.15	-.03(.03)	-.04	-.06(.03)*	-.09
Anger at Biden (Cross-Lagged)	-.07(.03)*	-.10	-.11(.03)***	-.14	-.10(.04)***	-.14	-.03(.03)	-.05

Between Person Correlation

Conservative Media Use-Anger	.58***	.59***	.59***	.59***
Anger-Belief Accuracy	−.56***	−.67***	−.68***	−.41***
Conservative Media Use-Belief Accuracy	−.38***	−.51***	−.50***	−.23***
Fit Indices				
RMSEA	.04	.04	.02	.03
CFI	1.00	1.00	1.00	1.00
TLI	.99	.99	1.00	1.00
χ^2 (df)	29.63(12)	29.58(12)	15.57(12)	25.04(12)

Note. *** $p < .001$, ** $p < .01$, * $p < .05$, # $p < .10$. Reported standardized coefficients are the averaged path for W1-W2 and W2-W3 (see Orth et al., 2021 for details). Results from RI-CLPMs for each outcome variable. For belief accuracy, more accurate beliefs are coded higher.

Table A.8 Predicting Liberal Media Use, Anger at Trump, and Belief Accuracy

	Trump China research		Trump Russia tape		Trump strokes		Trump mail	
	b (s.e.)	β	b (s.e.)	β	b (s.e.)	β	b (s.e.)	β
Effects on Liberal Media Use								
Liberal Media Use (Autoregressive)	.18(.06)**	.18	.18(.06)**	.18	.18(.06)**	.18	.18(.06)**	.18
Anger at Trump (Cross-Lagged)	−.06(.08)	−.05	−.03(.08)	−.02	−.03(.08)	−.02	−.07(.08)	−.05
Belief Accuracy (Cross-Lagged)	.01(.05)	.01	.17(.08)*	.10	.17(.08)*	.10	.06(.08)	.04
Effects on Anger at Trump								
Anger at Trump (Autoregressive)	.08(.12)	.08	.16(.11)	.16	.16(.11)	.16	.01(.11)	.01
Liberal Media Use (Cross-Lagged)	−.03(.05)	−.03	−.01(.05)	−.02	−.01(.05)	−.02	−.04(.05)	−.05
Belief Accuracy (Cross-Lagged)	.04(.05)	.05	−.12(.09)	−.09	.17(.08)	−.09	.06(.08)	−.01
Effects on Belief Accuracy								
Belief Accuracy (Autoregressive)	.18(.05)***	.18	.20(.07)**	.19	.20(.07)**	.19	.19(.07)**	.18
Liberal Media Use (Cross-Lagged)	.04(.04)	.05	.05(.03)#	.17	.05(.03)#	.08	.05(.03)	.08
Anger at Trump (Cross-Lagged)	.06(.06)	.05	.01(.05)	.01	.01(.05)	.01	−.04(.06)	−.04

Between Person Correlation				
Liberal Media Use-Anger	.67***	.68***	.68***	.67***
Anger-Belief Accuracy	−.77***	−.77***	−.77***	−.89***
Liberal Media Use-Belief Accuracy	−.54***	−.53***	−.53***	−.66***
Fit Indices				
RMSEA	.04	.05	.05	.02
CFI	1.00	1.00	1.00	1.00
TLI	.99	.99	.99	1.00
χ^2 (df)	36.75(12)	44.94(12)	44.94(12)	17.42(12)

Note. *** $p < .001$, ** $p < .01$, * $p < .05$, # $p < .10$. Reported standardized coefficients are the averaged path for W1-W2 and W2-W3 (see Orth et al., 2021 for details). Results from RI-CLPMs for each outcome variable. For belief accuracy, more accurate beliefs are coded higher.

References

Andersen, K., de Vreese, C., & Albæk, E. (2016). Measuring media diet in a high-choice environment-testing the list-frequency technique. *Communication Methods and Measures*, *10*(2–3), 81–98. https://doi.org/10.1080/19312458.2016.1150973.

Arceneaux, K., & Johnson, M. (2013). *Changing minds or changing channels? Partisan news in an age of choice*. University of Chicago Press.

Arguedas, R. A., Robertson, C., Fletcher, R., & Nielsen, R. (2022). *Echo chambers, filter bubbles, and polarization: A literature review*. Reuters Institute for the Study of Journalism.

Arpan, L. M., & Nabi, R. L. (2011). Exploring anger in the hostile media process: Effects on news preferences and source evaluation. *Journalism & Mass Communication Quarterly*, *88*(1), 5–22. https://doi.org/10.1177/107769901108800101.

Bakir, V., & McStay, A. (2018). Fake news and the economy of emotions: Problems, causes, and solutions. *Digital Journalism*, *6*(2), 154–175. https://doi.org/10.1080/21670811.2017.1345645.

Baum, M. A., & Groeling, T. (2008). New media and the polarization of American political discourse. *Political Communication*, *25*(4), 345–365. https://doi.org/10.1080/10584600802426965.

Baumgartner, S. E., van der Schuur, W. A., Lemmens, J. S., & te Poel, F. (2018). The relationship between media multitasking and attention problems in adolescents: Results of two longitudinal studies. *Human Communication Research*, *44*(1), 3–30. https://doi.org/10.1093/hcre.12111.

Benkler, Y., Faris, R., & Roberts, H. (2018). *Network propaganda: Manipulation, disinformation, and radicalization in American politics*. Oxford University Press.

Bennett, W. L., & Iyengar, S. (2008). A new era of minimal effects? The changing foundations of political communication. *Journal of Communication*, *58*(4), 707–731. https://doi.org/10.1111/j.1460-2466.2008.00410.x.

Bennett, W. L., & Livingston, S. (2018). The disinformation order: Disruptive communication and the decline of democratic institutions. *European Journal of communication*, *33*(2), 122–139. https://doi.org/10.1177/0267323118760317.

Berry, J. M., & Sobieraj, S. (2013). *The outrage industry: Political opinion media and the new incivility*. Oxford University Press.

Boyer, M. (2023). Aroused argumentation: How the news exacerbates motivated reasoning. *The International Journal of Press/Politics*, *28*(1), 92–115. https://doi.org/10.1177/19401612211010577.

Brock, D., Rabin-Havt, A., & Media Matters for America. (2012). *The Fox effect: How Roger Ailes turned a network into a propaganda machine.* Anchor Books.

Broockman, D. E., & Kalla, J. L. (2023). Consuming cross-cutting media causes learning and moderates attitudes: A field experiment with Fox News viewers. *Unpublished manuscript.* https://osf.io/preprints/osf/jrw26.

Budak, C., Goel, S., & Rao, J. M. (2016). Fair and balanced? Quantifying media bias through crowdsourced content analysis. *Public Opinion Quarterly, 80* (S1), 250–271. https://doi.org/10.1093/poq/nfw007.

Carnahan, D., Ahn, S., & Turner, M. M. (2023). The madness of misperceptions: Evaluating the ways anger contributes to misinformed beliefs. *Journal of Communication, 73*(1), 60–72. https://doi.org/10.1093/joc/jqac041.

Carver, C. S., & Harmon-Jones, E. (2009). Anger is an approach-related affect: Evidence and implications. *Psychological Bulletin, 135*, 183–204. https://doi.org/10.1037/a0013965.

Douglas, K. M., Uscinski, J. E., Sutton, R. M. et al. (2019). Understanding conspiracy theories. *Advances in Political Psychology, 40*(S1), 3–35. https://doi.org/10.1111/pops.12568.

Druckman, J. N., Levendusky, M. S., & McLain, A. (2018). No need to watch: How the effects of partisan media can spread via interpersonal discussions. *American Journal of Political Science, 62*, 99–112. https://doi.org/10.1111/ajps.12325.

Eady, G., Bonneau, R., Tucker, J. A., & Nagler, J. (2020). News sharing on social media: Mapping the ideology of news media content, citizens, and politicians. *OSF Preprint.* https://doi.org/10.31219/osf.io/ch8gj.

Enders, A. M., Uscinski, J. E., Klofstad, C. A. et al. (2022). Who supports QAnon? A case study in political extremism. *Journal of Politics, 84*(3), 1844–1849. https://doi.org/10.1086/717850.

Famulari, U. (2020). Framing the Trump administration's "zero tolerance" policy: A quantitative content analysis of news stories and visuals in US news websites. *Journalism Studies, 21*(16), 2267–2284. https://doi.org/10.1080/1461670X.2020.1832141.

Faris, R., Roberts, H., Etling, B. et al. (2017). *Partisanship, propaganda, and disinformation: Online media and the 2016 U.S. presidential election.* Berkman Klein Center Research.

Feldman, L., Maibach, E. W., Roser-Renouf, C., & Leiserowitz, A. (2012). Climate on cable: The nature and impact of global warming coverage on Fox

News, CNN, and MSNBC. *The International Journal of Press/Politics, 17* (1), 3–31. https://doi.org/10.1177/1940161211425410.

Feldman, L., Myers, T. A., Hmielowski, J. D., & Lieserowitz, A. (2014). The mutual reinforcement of media selectivity and effects: Testing the reinforcing spirals framework in the context of global warming. *Journal of Communication, 64*(4), 590–611. https://doi.org/10.1111/jcom.12108.

Fletcher, R., Robertson, C. T., & Nielsen, R. K. (2021). How many people live in politically partisan online news echo chambers in different countries? *Journal of Quantitative Description: Digital Media, 1*, 1–56. https://doi .org/10.51685/jqd.2021.020.

Flynn, D. J., Nyhan, B., & Reifler, J. (2017). The nature and origins of misperceptions: Understanding false and unsupported beliefs about politics. *Political Psychology, 38*, 127–150. https://doi.org/10.1111/pops.12394.

Garrett, R. K. (2009). Politically motivated reinforcement seeking: Reframing the selective exposure debate. *Journal of communication, 59*(4), 676–699. https://doi.org/10.1111/j.1460-2466.2009.01452.x.

Garrett, R. K., & Bond, R. M. (2021). Conservative' susceptibility to political misperceptions. *Science Advances, 7*(23), 1–9. https://doi.org/10.1126/ sciadv.abf1234.

Garrett, R. K., Long, J. A., & Jeong, M. S. (2019). From partisan media to misperception: Affective polarization as mediator. *Journal of Communication, 69*(5), 490–512. https://doi.org/10.1093/joc/jqz028.

Garrett, R. K., & Stroud, N. J. (2014). Partisan paths to exposure diversity: Differences in pro-and counterattitudinal news consumption. *Journal of Communication, 64*(4), 680–701. https://doi.org/10.1111/jcom.12105.

Garrett, R. K., Weeks, B. E., & Neo, R. L. (2016). Driving a wedge between evidence and beliefs: How online ideological news exposure promotes political misperceptions. *Journal of Computer-Mediated Communication, 21*(5), 31–348. https://doi.org/10.1111/jcc4.12164.

González-Bailón, S., Lazer, D., Barberá, P. et al. (2023). Asymmetric ideological segregation in exposure to political news on Facebook. *Science, 381*, 392–398. https://doi.org/10.1126/science.ade7138.

Goodall, C. E., Slater, M. D., & Myers, T. A. (2013). Fear and anger responses to local news coverage of alcohol-related crimes, accidents, and injuries: Explaining news effects of policy support using a representative sample of messages and people. *Journal of Communication, 63*(2), 373–392. https:// doi.org/10.1111/jcom.12020.

Graham, M. H. (2023). Measuring misperceptions? *American Political Science Review, 117*(1), 80–102. https://doi.org/10.1017/S0003055422000387.

Gross, K., & Brewer, P. R. (2007). Sore losers: News frames, policy debates, and emotions. *Harvard International Journal of Press/Politics*, *12*(1), 122–133. https://doi.org/10.1177/1081180X06297231.

Guess, A. M. (2021). (Almost) everything in moderation: New evidence on Americans' online media diets. *American Journal of Political Science*, *65*(4), 1007–1022. https://doi.org/10.1111/ajps.12589.

Guess, A. M., Barberá, P., Munzert, S., & Yang, J. (2021). The consequences of online partisan media. *Proceedings of the National Academy of Sciences*, *118* (14), 1–8. https://doi.org/10.1073/pnas.2013464118.

Hamaker, E. L., Kuiper, R. M., & Grasman, R. P. P. P. (2015). A critique of the cross-lagged panel model. *Psychological Methods*, *20*(1), 102–116. https://doi.org/10.1037/a0038889.

Harber, J., Singh, L., Budak, C. et al. (2021). Lies and presidential debates: How political misinformation spread across media streams during the 2020 election. *Harvard Kennedy School Misinformation Review*, *2*(6), 1–38. https://doi.org/10.37016/mr-2020-84.

Hasell, A. (2021). Shared emotion: The social amplification of partisan news on twitter. *Digital Journalism*, *9*(8), 1085–1102. https://doi.org/10.1080/21670811.2020.1831937.

Hasell, A., Halversen, A., & Weeks, B. E. (2024). When social media attack: How exposure to political attacks on social media promotes anger and political cynicism. *International Journal of Press/Politics*. Advance online publication. https://doi.org/10.1177/19401612231221806.

Hasell, A., & Weeks, B. E. (2016). Partisan provocation: The role of partisan news use and emotional responses in political information sharing in social media. *Human Communication Research*, *42*(4), 641–661. https://doi.org/10.1111/hcre.12092.

Hemmer, N. (2016). *Messengers of the right: Conservative media and the transformation of American politics*. University of Pennsylvania Press.

Hiaeshutter-Rice, D., & Weeks, B. (2021). Understanding audience engagement with mainstream and alternative news posts on Facebook. *Digital Journalism*, *9*(5), 519–548. https://doi.org/10.1080/21670811.2021.1924068.

Hmielowski, J. D., Hutchens, M. J., & Beam, M. A. (2020). Asymmetry of partisan media effects? Examining the reinforcing process of conservative and liberal media with political beliefs. *Political Communication*, *37*(6), 852–868. https://doi.org/10.1080/10584609.2020.1763525.

Hmielowski, J. D., Staggs, S., Hutchens, M. J., & Beam, M. A. (2022). Talking politics: The relationship between supportive and opposing discussion with partisan media credibility and use. *Communication Research*, *49*(2), 221–244. https://doi.org/10.1177/0093650220915041.

Holt, K., Figenschou, T. U., & Frischlich, L. (2019). Key dimensions of alternative news media. *Digital Journalism, 7*(7), 860–869. https://doi.org/10.1080/21670811.2019.1625715.

Hsu, T., & Robertson, K. (2021). You can barely tell it's the same trial in cable impeachment coverage. *The New York Times.* www.nytimes.com/2021/02/12/business/media/cnn-fox-news-msnbc-impeachment-trial.html.

Internet Archive TV News. (2022). https://archive.org/details/tv.

Iyengar, S., & Hahn, K. S. (2009). Red media, blue media: Evidence of ideological selectivity in media use. *Journal of Communication, 59*(1), 19–39. https://doi.org/10.1111/j.1460-2466.2008.01402.x.

Iyengar, S., Lelkes, Y., Levendusky, M., Malhotra, N., & Westwood, S. J. (2019). The origins and consequences of affective polarization in the United States. *Annual Review of Political Science, 22*, 129–146. https://doi.org/10.1146/annurev-polisci-051117-073034.

Jack, C. (2017). *Lexicon of lies: Terms for problematic information.* Data & Society.

Jamieson, K. H. (2020). *Cyberwar: How Russian hackers and trolls helped elect a president: What we do 't, ca 't, and do know.* Oxford University Press.

Jamieson, K. H., & Cappella, J. N. (2008). *Echo chamber: Rush Limbaugh and the conservative media establishment.* Oxford University Press.

Jamieson, K. H., Levendusky, M., Pasek, J. et al. (2023). *Democracy amid crises: Polarization, pandemic, protests, and persuasion.* Oxford University Press.

Lee, J. (2020). Is USPS purposefully slowing mail to help reelect Trump? *Snopes.* www.snopes.com/fact-check/usps-slowing-mail-trump/.

Levendusky, M. S. (2013). Why do partisan media polarize viewers? *American Journal of Political Science, 57*, 611–623. https://doi.org/10.1111/ajps.12008.

Lu, Y., & Lee, J. K. (2019). Partisan information sources and affective polarization: Panel analysis of the mediating role of anger and fear. *Journalism & Mass Communication Quarterly, 96*(3), 767–783. https://doi.org/10.1177/1077699018811295.

MacKuen, M., Wolak, J., Keele, L., & Marcus, G. E. (2010). Civic engagements: Resolute partisanship or reflective deliberation. *American Journal of Political Science, 54*(2), 440–458. https://doi.org/10.1111/j.1540-5907.2010.00440.x.

Marcus, G. E., Neuman, W. R., & MacKuen, M. (2000). *Affective intelligence and political judgment.* University of Chicago Press.

Marwick, A. E., & Lewis, R. (2017). *Media manipulation and disinformation online.* Data and Society Research Institute.

Mason, L. (2016). A cross-cutting calm: How social sorting drives affective polarization. *Public Opinion Quarterly, 80*(S1), 351–377. https://doi.org/10.1093/poq/nfw001.

McCann Ramirez, N. (2022). Timeline: Tucker Carlson's unhinged COVID-19 coverage. *Media Matters for America.* August 15, 2023, www.mediamatters.org/tucker-carlson/timeline-tucker-carlsons-unhinged-covid-19-coverage.

Meirick, P. C. (2013). Motivated misperception? Party, education, partisan news, and belief in "death panels". *Journalism & Mass Communication Quarterly, 90*(1), 39–57. https://doi.org/10.1177/1077699012468696.

Metzger, M. J., Hartsell, E. H., & Flanagin, A. J. (2020). Cognitive dissonance or credibility? A comparison of two theoretical explanations for selective exposure to partisan news. *Communication Research, 47*(1), 3–28. https://doi.org/10.1177/0093650215613136.

Monmouth University. (2022). *National: Faith in American system recovers after summer Jan. 6 hearings.* www.monmouth.edu/polling-institute/documents/monmouthpoll_us_092722.pdf/. *6 hearings.* www.monmouth.edu/polling-institute/documents/monmouthpoll_us_092722.pdf/.

Motta, M., & Stecula, D. (2023). The effects of partisan media in the face of global pandemic: How news shaped COVID-19 vaccine hesitancy. *Political Communication, 40,* 1–22. https://doi.org/10.1080/10584609.2023.2187496.

Motta, M., Stecula, D., & Farhart, C. (2020). How right-leaning media coverage of COVID-19 facilitated the spread of misinformation in the early stages of the pandemic in the US. *Canadian Journal of Political Science/Revueolarizatie de science politique, 53*(2), 335–342. https://doi.org/10.1017/S0008423920000396.

Muise, D., Hosseinmardi, H., Howland, B. et al. (2022). Quantifying partisan news diets in Web and TV audiences. *Science Advances, 8*(28), 1–11. https://doi.org/10.1126/sciadv.abn0083.

Mulder, J. D., & Hamaker, E. L. (2021). Three extensions of the random intercept cross-lagged panel model. *Structural Equation Modeling: A Multidisciplinary Journal, 28*(4), 638–648. https://doi.org/10.1080/10705511.2020.1784738.

Mutz, D. C. (2016). *In-your-face politics: The consequences of uncivil media.* Princeton University Press.

Nabi, R. L. (2003). Exploring the framing effects of emotion: Do discrete emotions differentially influence information accessibility, information seeking, and policy preference? *Communication Research, 30*(2), 224–247. https://doi.org/10.1177/0093650202250881.

Orth, U., Clark., D. A., Donnellan, M. B., & Robins, R. W. (2021). Testing prospective effects in longitudinal research: Comparing seven competing cross-lagged models. *Journal of Personality and Social Psychology, 120*(4), 1013–1034. https://doi.org/10.1037/pspp0000358.

Pariser, E. (2011). *The filter bubble: What the internet is hiding from you.* The Penguin Press.

Patterson, T. E. (2016). News coverage of the 2016 general election: How the press failed the voters. *HKS Working Paper No. RWP16-052.*

Peck, R. (2019). *Fox populism: Branding conservatism as working class.* Cambridge University Press.

Peck, A. (2020). A problem of amplification: Folklore and fake news in the age of social media. *Journal of American Folklore, 133*(529), 329–351. https://doi.org/10.5406/jamerfolk.133.529.0329.

Peck, R. (2023). Comparing populist media: From Fox News to the Young Turks, from cable to YouTube, from right to left. *Television & New Media, 24*, 599–615. https://doi.org/10.1177/15274764221114349.

Pew Research Center. (2020a). *Americans' main sources for political news vary by party and age.* www.pewresearch.org/short-reads/2020/04/01/americans-main-sources-for-political-news-vary-by-party-and-age/.

Pew Research Center. (2020b). *U.S. media polarization and the 2020 election: A nation divided.* www.pewresearch.org/journalism/2020/01/24/u-s-media-polarization-and-the-2020-election-a-nation-divided/.

Pew Research Center. (2020). *A look at the Americans who believe there is some truth to the conspiracy theory that COVID-19 was planned.* www.pewresearch.org/short-reads/2020/07/24/a-look-at-the-americans-who-believe-there-is-some-truth-to-the-conspiracy-theory-that-covid-19-was-planned/.

Pew Research Center. (2021). *Partisan divides in media trust widen, driven by a decline among Republicans.* www.pewresearch.org/short-reads/2021/08/30/partisan-divides-in-media-trust-widen-driven-by-a-decline-among-republicans/.

Pew Research Center. (2023). *Demographic profiles of Republican and Democratic voters.* www.pewresearch.org/politics/2023/07/12/demographic-profiles-of-republican-and-democratic-voters/.

Phoenix, D. L. (2020). *The anger gap: How race shapes emotion in politics.* Cambridge University Press.

Prior, M. (2013). Media and political polarization. *Annual Review of Political Science, 16*, 101–127. https://doi.org/10.1146/annurev-polisci-100711-135242.

Puglisi, R., & Snyder Jr., J. M. (2011). Newspaper coverage of political scandals. *The Journal of Politics, 73*(3), 931–950. https://doi.org/10.1017/S0022381611000569.

Roberts, J., & Wahl-Jorgensen, K. (2022). Reporting the news: How Breitbart derives legitimacy from recontextualized news. *Discourse & Society*, 33, 833–846. https://doi.org/10.1177/09579265221095422.

Savillo, R., & Monroe, T. (2021). *Fox's effort to undermine vaccines has only worsened*. Media Matters for America. August 15, 2023, www.mediamatters .org/fox-news/foxs-effort-undermine-vaccines-has-only-worsened.

Scharkow, M. (2019). The reliability and temporal stability of self-reported media exposure: A meta-analysis. *Communication Methods and Measures*, *13*(3), 198–211. https://doi.org/10.1080/19312458.2019.1594742.

Schnauber-Stockmann, A., Weber, M., Reinecke, L. et al. (2021). Mobile (self-) socialization: The role of mobile media and communication in autonomy and relationship development in adolescence. *Mass Communication and Society*, *24*(6), 867–891. https://doi.org/10.1080/15205436.2021.1964538.

Shah, D. V., McLeod, D. M., Rojas, H. et al. (2017). Revising the communication mediation model for a new political communication ecology. *Human Communication Research*, *43*(4), 491–504. https://doi.org/10.1111/hcre.12115.

Shehata, A., Thomas, F., Glogger, I., & Ansdersen, K. (2024). Belief maintenance as a media effect: A conceptualization and empirical approach. *Human Communication Research*, *50*(1), 1–13. https://doi.org/10.1093/hcr/hqad033.

Shultziner, D., & Stukalin, Y. (2021). Politicizing what's news: How partisan media bias occurs in news production. *Mass Communication and Society*, *24* (3), 372–393. https://doi.org/10.1080/15205436.2020.1812083.

Slater, M. D. (2007). Reinforcing spirals: The mutual influence of media selectivity and media effects and their impact on individual behavior and social identity. *Communication Theory*, *17*(3), 281–303. https://doi.org/10.1111/j.1468-2885.2007.00296.x.

Slater, M. D., Shehata, A., & Strömbäck, J. (2020). Reinforcing spirals model. In J. Van den Bulck, D. R. Ewoldsen, M.-L. Mares, & E. Scharrer (Eds.), *International encyclopedia of media psychology*. John Wiley & Sons. https://onlinelibrary.wiley.com/doi/full/10.1002/9781119011071.iemp0134.

Smith, B. (2020). Jeff Zucker helped create Donald Trump. That show may be ending. *The New York Times*. www.nytimes.com/2020/09/20/business/media/jeff-zucker-helped-create-donald-trump-that-show-may-be-ending .html.

Song, H. (2017). Why do people (sometimes) become selective about news? The role of emotions and partisan differences in selective approach and avoidance. *Mass Communication and Society*, *20*, 47–67. https://doi.org/10.1080/15205436.2016.1187755.

Stroud, N. J. (2011). *Niche news: The politics of news choice*. Oxford University Press.

Sunstein, C. R. (2007). *Republic.com 2.0*. Princeton University Press.

Television Archive. (n.d.). https://archive.org/details/tvarchive.

Thomas, F., Shehata, A., Otto, L. P., Möller, J., & Prestele, E. (2021). How to capture reciprocal communication dynamics: Comparing longitudinal statistical approaches in order to analyze within- and between-person effects. *Journal of Communication, 71*(2), 187–219. https://doi.org/10.1093/joc/jqab003.

Thorson, K., & Wells, C. (2016). Curated flows: A framework for mapping media exposure in the digital age. *Communication Theory, 26*(3), 309–328. https://doi.org/10.1111/comt.12087.

Tsfati, Y., & Cappella, J. N. (2003). Do people watch what they do not trust? Exploring the associations between news media skepticism and exposure. *Communication Research, 30*, 504–529. https://doi.org/10.1177/0093650203253371.

Vargo. C. J., Guo, L., & Amazeen, M. A. (2018). The agenda-setting power of fake news: A big data analysis of the online media landscape from 2014 to 2016. *New Media & Society, 20*(5), 2028–2049. https://doi.org/10.1177/1461444817712086.

Vraga, E. K., & Bode, L. (2020). Defining misinformation and understanding its bounded nature: Using expertise and evidence for describing misinformation. *Political Communication, 37*(1), 136–144. https://doi.org/10.1080/10584609.2020.1716500.

Wahl-Jorgensen, K. (2019). *Emotions, media and politics*. John Wiley & Sons.

Webster, S. W. (2020). *American rage: How anger shapes our politics*. Cambridge University Press.

Weeks, B. E. (2015). Emotions, partisanship, and misperceptions: How anger and anxiety moderate the effect of partisan bias on susceptibility to political misinformation. *Journal of Communication, 65*(4), 699–719. https://doi.org/10.1111/jcom.12164.

Weeks, B. E. (2023). Emotion, digital media, and misinformation. In R. L. Nabi and J. G. Myrick (Eds.), *Emotions in the digital world: Exploring affective experiences and expression in online interactions* (pp. 422–442). Oxford University Press.

Weeks, B. E., Menchen-Trevino, E., Calabrese, C., Casas, A., & Wojcieszak, M. (2023). Partisan media, untrustworthy news sites, and political misperceptions. *New Media & Society, 25*, 2644–2662. https://doi.org/10.1177/1461444821103330.

Weeks, B., & Southwell, B. (2010). The symbiosis of news coverage and aggregate online search behavior. Obama, rumors, and presidential politics. *Mass Communication and Society, 13*, 341–360. https://doi.org/10/1080/15205430903470532.

Wells, C., Shah, D., Lukito, J. et al. (2020). Trump, Twitter, and news media responsiveness: A media systems approach. *New Media & Society, 22*, 659–682.

Wojcieszak, M. (2021). What predicts selective exposure online: Testing political attitudes, credibility, and social identity. *Communication Research, 48* (5), 687–716. https://doi.org/10.1177/0093650219844868.

Wojcieszak, M., Bimber, B., Feldman, L., & Stroud, N. J. (2016). Partisan news and political participation: Exploring mediated relationships. *Political Communication, 33*(2), 241–260. https://doi.org/10.1080/10584609.2015.1051608.

Wojcieszak, M., de Leeuw, S., Menchen-Trevino, E. et al. (2023). No polarization from partisan news: Over-time evidence from trace data. *International Journal of Press/Politics, 28*(3), 601–626. https://doi.org/10.1177/19401612211047194.

Young, D. G. (2019). *Irony and outrage: The polarized landscape of rage, fear, and laughter in the United States*. Oxford University Press.

Young, D. G. (2023). *Wrong: How media, politics, and identity drive our appetite for misinformation*. Johns Hopkins University Press.

Zhang, Y., Chen, F., & Lukito, J. (2023). Network amplification of politicized information and misinformation about COVID-19 by conservative media and partisan influencers on Twitter. *Political Communication, 40*, 24–47. https://doi.org/10.1080/10584609.2022.2113844.

Acknowledgments

I would like to thank the following individuals and groups for their comments, suggestions, critiques, questions, advice, support, or encouragement on this project. I sincerely appreciate Kim Andersen, Michael Beam, Ceren Budak, Susan Douglas, Jessica Feezell, Richard Fletcher, Kelly Garrett, Ruth and Gary Hasell, Matt Hindman, Lance Holbert, Josh Pasek, Robin Queen, Christian Schemer, Adam Shehata, Nikki Usher, Cristian Vaccari, Ed Weeks, Danna Young, members of the University of Michigan's Political Communication Working Group, attendees at the 2023 International Journal of Press/Politics conference, and two anonymous reviewers. I am also very thankful to Julia Lippman for research assistance with the project. I would particularly like to thank Ariel Hasell for talking through ideas, reading and editing drafts, and generally improving my work. Finally, many thanks to Stuart Soroka for encouraging me to pursue this Element, which was a fun departure from journal articles. I greatly appreciate Stuart's patience and flexibility during this entire process, as well as his mentorship and guidance. This work was supported in part by the University of Michigan's College of Literature, Science, and the Arts Associate Professor Support Fund, as well as the Department of Communication & Media and the Center for Political Studies at UM.

Cambridge Elements ☰

Politics and Communication

Stuart Soroka
University of California

Stuart Soroka is a Professor in the Department of Communication at the University of California, Los Angeles, and Adjunct Research Professor at the Center for Political Studies at the Institute for Social Research, University of Michigan. His research focuses on political communication, political psychology, and the relationships between public policy, public opinion, and mass media. His books with Cambridge University Press include The Increasing Viability of Good News (2021, with Yanna Krupnikov), Negativity in Democratic Politics (2014), Information and Democracy (forthcoming, with Christopher Wlezien) and Degrees of Democracy (2010, with Christopher Wlezien).

About the series

Cambridge Elements in Politics and Communication publishes research focused on the intersection of media, technology, and politics. The series emphasizes forward-looking reviews of the field, path-breaking theoretical and methodological innovations, and the timely application of social-scientific theory and methods to current developments in politics and communication around the world.

Cambridge Elements ☰

Politics and Communication

Elements in the Series

A full series listing is available at: www.cambridge.org/EPCM

.

Printed in the United States
by Baker & Taylor Publisher Services